MILITARY POWER

82ND
AIRBORNE

FRED PUSHIES

ZENITH PRESS

First published in 2008 by Zenith Press, an imprint of MBI Publishing Company, 400 1st Avenue North, Suite 300, Minneapolis, MN 55401 USA.

© Fred Pushies, 2008

Zenith Press titles are also available at discounts in bulk quantity for industrial or sales-promotional use. For details write to Special Sales Manager at MBI Publishing Company, 400 1st Avenue North, Suite 300, Minneapolis, MN 55401 USA.

To find out more about our books, join us online at www.zenithpress.com.

On the cover: Soldiers from the 82nd Airborne Division parachute over Andrews Air Force Base, Maryland, during a joint-service open house. *U.S. Army photo by Staff Sgt. Jason W. Edwards*

On the frontispiece: Taking back the streets, the "Black Falcons" put boots on the ground in Iraq. Staff Sgt. Steven Michaelis, a squad leader from Battery B, 2nd Battalion, 319th Airborne Field Artillery Regiment, 2nd Brigade Combat Team, takes the point as his platoon moves down a street in Adhamiyah. *Sgt. Michael Pryor*

On the title page: U.S. Army soldiers breach a house to search for insurgent activities during an operation in Zaghiniyat, Iraq. The mission is to rid an area of insurgent forces and allow coalition forces freedom of movement throughout the area of operations. The soldiers are with Charlie Troop, 5th Squadron, 73rd Cavalry Regiment, 82nd Airborne Division. *Staff Sgt. Joann Makinano*

On the back cover, top right: Sgt. Michael Gurley, flight engineer for Company B, 3rd General Support Aviation Battalion, 82nd Combat Aviation Brigade, scans the terrain for activity from the opening of a CH-47 Chinook. *Pfc. Aubree Rundle*

Bottom right: Spc. Martin Garza, an artilleryman with Battery B, 2nd Battalion, 319th Airborne Field Artillery Regiment, 2nd Brigade Combat Team, and a fellow paratrooper patrol Adhamiyah, Iraq, which is known as a hot spot for improvised explosive devices (IEDs). Using cover and concealment, the pair of troopers keep a watchful eye out for insurgents. *Sgt. Michael Pryor*

About the author:
Fred Pushies has spent the last seventeen years in the company of units assigned to U.S. Special Operations Command (SOCOM). He has skimmed across the waves with the SEALs in an eighty-two-foot-long Mark V Special Operations craft, flown at treetop level with the 160th Special Operations Aviation Regiment, and crunched through the brush with Force Recon Marines. His integrity and insight are evident in his previous works, *Special Ops: America's Elite Forces in 21st Century Combat, U.S. Air Force Special Ops, U.S. Army Special Forces, Marine Force Recon,* and *Weapons of the U.S. Navy SEALs.*

Library of Congress Cataloging-in-Publication Data

Pushies, Fred J., 1952–
    82nd Airborne / Fred Pushies.
        p. cm.
    Includes index.
    ISBN 978-0-7603-3465-2 (pbk. : alk. paper)
    1. United States. Army. Airborne Division, 82nd—History. I. Title.
    UA27.582nd P87 2008
    356'.16630973—dc22

2008007884

Designer: Brenda C. Canales

Printed in Singapore

Contents

Chapter 1

HISTORY

Camp Gordon, Georgia, established on 25 August 1917, was the home of the 82nd Infantry Division during World War I. Men from all over the United States assembled at this camp, earning the 82nd the nickname the "All American" Division. The double "A" insignia created for the division is still in use today. *82nd Airborne Division War Memorial Museum, Fort Bragg, North Carolina*

The 82nd Airborne Division began its legendary entrance into the annals of military history with the formation of the 82nd Infantry Division during World War I. On 25 August 1917, the division was formed at Camp Gordon, located just southwest of Augusta, Georgia.

Men from every corner of the United States were assembled at Camp Gordon, which earned the newly created unit the nickname the "All American" Division. This moniker remains to this day and is carried through on the division's famous "AA" shoulder patch.

Supplies, uniforms, and weapons were scarce as the unit filled its ranks. The men made do with what they had as the cadre transformed civilians into soldiers. In April 1918

the orders came to prepare for embarkation to Europe. The 82nd Infantry Division was going to war.

In June 1918 the division took its position in the Toul section of France fighting against the "Hun." During this summer the 82nd would experience life in the trenches as it relieved soldiers from the 26th Division. In August the 82nd was relieved by elements of the 89th Division, giving the 89th two months of service on the line.

After a short rest, the 82nd was again placed on the line as it moved to the Marabache sector. Its orders were to conduct patrols and occupy the area located along the Selle River, in the Moselle River Valley.

In September 1918 the first American offensive, planned and conducted by the Americans, was launched.

A soldier sights in his M1 Garand rifle during a training exercise. Gen. George S. Patton commented that the M1 was "the greatest battle implement ever devised." The M1 was a .30-caliber semi-automatic rifle with an eight-round clip. The rifle had an effective range of 500 yards. This soldier uses his bicycle for what little cover it provides. *82nd Airborne Division War Memorial Museum, Fort Bragg, North Carolina*

Soldiers of the 82nd Airborne Division in training, armed with a machine gun. The Browning M1919A4 is a fully automatic air-cooled weapon chambered in .30 caliber. The ammunition is belt-fed on a 250-round fabric belt. Much lighter than the .20-caliber water-cooled M1917A1 machine gun, the M1919A4 had an effective range of 1,100 yards with a rate of fire of five hundred rounds per minute. *82nd Airborne Division War Memorial Museum, Fort Bragg, North Carolina*

Members of the 82nd Airborne Division's 325th Glider Infantry Regiment (GIR) perform final checks as they prepare for takeoff. Augmenting the paratroopers, the GIR flew into battle in Waco gliders. The gliders were towed behind C-47 transport aircraft; once the aircraft reached their landing area, the gliders were cut loose from the towline. Seen here on the gliders are the black and white stripes identifying them as Allied aircraft. *82nd Airborne Division War Memorial Museum, Fort Bragg, North Carolina*

The mission was to attack the fortified town of St. Mihiel. The French army had made several attempts to rout the Germans, with no success. It was now up to the Americans and the 82nd Infantry Division. One night during this operation, the Germans introduced the doughboys to chemical warfare as they began an artillery barrage of mustard gas. When the sun rose the next morning, the soldiers of the 82nd had held the line and accomplished their mission.

The last major American offensive of the war took place in the Argonne Forest in preparation for an invasion of Germany. The division battled for more than a week, eventually punching a hole in the enemy's line and creating a corridor for Allied forces to proceed on to the "Fatherland."

By the end of World War I, the 82nd Infantry Division had engaged the enemy in three major campaigns in the span of five months. After the Great War, the unit returned to the States and was demobilized.

A group of paratroopers digs in and prepares a fighting position during the Normandy invasion. A Browning automatic rifle (BAR) can be seen on the edge of one of the many hedgerows of the French countryside. Another soldier is working on a foxhole. *82nd Airborne Division War Memorial Museum, Fort Bragg, North Carolina*

Members of the 82nd Airborne Division's 3rd Brigade construct bunkers during the Vietnam War. The brigade was deployed to Southeast Asia for two years. *82nd Airborne Division War Memorial Museum, Fort Bragg, North Carolina*

On 25 March 1942, about three months after Japan's attack on Pearl Harbor, the 82nd Infantry Division was reactivated. The division, now located at Camp Claiborne, Louisiana, was under the command of Maj. Gen. Omar Bradley. Subsequently, on 15 August 1942, the unit became the army's first airborne infantry unit, redesignated as the 82nd Airborne Division, under the command of Maj. Gen. Matthew B. Ridgway.

At the same time, the 325th Glider Infantry Regiment (GIR) was formed, providing the Airborne delivery of jeeps, cannons, and other equipment to the battlefield. During the late summer of 1943, the 82nd Airborne paratroopers and glider troops took part in combat operations in Italy: Operation Husky in Sicily and Operations Avalanche and Oil Drum Drop in Salerno. It was during the Italian campaign that a German officer tagged the 504th Parachute Infantry Regiment with the nickname "Devils in Baggy Pants."

At the end of 1943, the 82nd Airborne left Italy and restaged in England in preparation for the liberation of Europe. Whereas the code name for the amphibious assault on Normandy was Overlord, the airborne assault was code named Operation Neptune. The 82nd was

The 82nd Airborne was called into action during the U.S. invasion of the island of Grenada. In October 1983 Operation Urgent Fury was conducted to rescue American students located on this small island in the Caribbean. Here a group of paratroopers transports rucksacks and equipment in a M151 military utility tactical truck (MUTT). *82nd Airborne Division War Memorial Museum, Fort Bragg, North Carolina*

reorganized for the mission with the addition of two new parachute infantry regiments (PIR): the 507th and the 508th. Although the 505th Parachute Infantry Regiment remained, the 504th Parachute Infantry Regiment was detached from the division at this time and did not take part in the operation.

On the evening of 5 June 1944, soldiers of the 82nd and 101st airborne divisions loaded onto C-47 transport planes. Along with the paratroopers were members of the 325th Glider Infantry Regiment; they were riding in Waco gliders attached to other C-47 transport aircraft for what would be the largest airborne assault in history. The drop zones were near the towns of St. Mere Eglise and Carentan. The paratroopers' mission was to secure the roadways leading back to the beachhead, preventing any German reinforcements.

That was the plan as the paratroopers led the Allied invasion into occupied France, a date known as D-Day. However—as any veteran will tell you—according to

continued on page 14

All American Division
Medal of Honor Citations

World War I:
Emory J. Pike*

Rank and organization: lieutenant colonel, U.S. Army, division machine-gun officer, 82nd Division. Place and date: Near Vandieres, France, 15 September 1918. Entered service at Des Moines, Iowa. Birth: Columbia City, Iowa. G.O. No. 16, W.D., 1919. Citation: Having gone forward to reconnoiter new machine-gun positions, Lieutenant Colonel Pike offered his assistance in reorganizing advance infantry units that had become disorganized during a heavy artillery shelling. He succeeded in locating only about twenty men, but with these he advanced, and when he was later joined by several infantry platoons, he rendered inestimable service in establishing outposts, encouraging all by his cheeriness, in spite of the extreme danger of the situation. When a shell wounded one of the men in the outpost, Lieutenant Colonel Pike immediately went to his aid; he was severely wounded himself when another shell burst in the same place. While waiting to be brought to the rear, Lieutenant Colonel Pike continued in command, still retaining his jovial manner of encouragement, directing the reorganization until the position could be held. The entire operation was carried on under terrific bombardment, and the example of courage and devotion to duty set by Lieutenant Colonel Pike established the highest standard of morale and confidence to all under his charge. The wounds he received were the cause of his death.

Alvin C. York

Rank and organization: corporal, U.S. Army, Company G, 328th Infantry, 82nd Division. Place and date: Near Chatel-Chehery, France, 8 October 1918. Entered service at Pall Mall, Tennessee. Born: 13 December 1887, Fentress County, Tennessee. G.O. No. 59, W.D., 1919. Citation: After his platoon had suffered heavy casualties and three other noncommissioned officers had become casualties, Corporal York assumed command. Fearlessly leading seven men, he charged with great daring a machine-gun nest that was pouring deadly and incessant fire upon his platoon. In this heroic feat the machine-gun nest was taken, together with 4 officers and 128 men and several guns.

World War II:
Charles N. DeGlopper*

Rank and organization: private first class, U.S. Army, Company C, 325th Glider Infantry, 82nd Airborne Division. Place and date: Merderet River at La Fiere, France, 9 June 1944. Entered service at Grand Island, New York. Birth: Grand Island, New York. G.O. No. 22, 28 February 1946. Citation: Private First Class DeGlopper, a member of Company C, 325th Glider Infantry, on 9 June 1944 was advancing with the forward platoon to secure a bridgehead across the Merderet River at La Fiere, France. At dawn the platoon had penetrated an outer line of machine guns and riflemen, but in so doing it had become cut off from the rest of the company. Vastly superior forces began a decimation of the stricken unit and put in motion a flanking maneuver that would have completely exposed the American platoon in a shallow roadside ditch where it had taken cover. Detecting this danger, Private First Class DeGlopper volunteered to support his comrades by fire from his automatic rifle while they attempted a withdrawal through a break in a hedgerow forty yards to the rear. Scorning a concentration of enemy automatic weapons and rifle fire, Private First Class DeGlopper walked from the ditch onto the road in full view of the Germans, and sprayed the hostile positions with assault fire. He was wounded, but he continued firing. Struck again, he started to fall; yet his grim determination and valiant fighting spirit could not be broken. Kneeling in the roadway, weakened by his grievous wounds, he leveled his heavy weapon against the enemy and fired burst after burst until he was killed outright. He was successful in drawing the enemy action away from his fellow soldiers, who continued the fight from a more advantageous position and established the first bridgehead over the Merderet. In the area where Private First Class DeGlopper made his intrepid stand, his comrades later found the ground strewn with dead Germans and many machine guns and automatic weapons that he had knocked out of action. Private First Class DeGlopper's gallant sacrifice and unflinching heroism while facing insurmountable odds were in great measure responsible for a highly important tactical victory in the Normandy campaign.

John R. Towle*

Rank and organization: private, U.S. Army, Company C, 504th Parachute Infantry, 82nd Airborne Division. Place and date: Near Oosterhout, Holland, 21 September 1944. Entered service at Cleveland, Ohio. Birth: Cleveland, Ohio. G.O. No. 18, 15 March 1945. Citation. For conspicuous gallantry and intrepidity at the risk of life above and beyond the call of duty on 21 September 1944, near Oosterhout, Holland. The rifle company in which Private Towle served as rocket launcher gunner was occupying a defensive position in the west sector of the recently established Nijmegen bridgehead when a strong enemy force of approximately a hundred infantry supported by two tanks and a half-track formed for a counterattack. With full knowledge of the disastrous consequences resulting not only to his company but to the entire bridgehead by an enemy breakthrough, Private Towle immediately and without orders left his foxhole and moved two hundred yards in the face of intense small-arms fire to a position on an exposed dike roadbed. From this precarious position, Private Towle fired his rocket launcher at both tanks to his immediate front. Although he hit them, armored skirting prevented penetration by the projectiles; however, both vehicles were slightly damaged as they withdrew. Still under intense fire and fully exposed to the enemy, Private Towle then engaged a nearby house that nine Germans had entered and were using as a strongpoint; with one round, Private Towle killed all nine men. Hurriedly replenishing his supply of ammunition, Private Towle, motivated only by his high concept of duty that called for the destruction of the enemy at any cost, then rushed approximately 125 yards through grazing enemy fire to an exposed position from which he could engage the enemy half-track with his rocket launcher. While in a kneeling position preparatory to firing on the enemy vehicle, Private Towle was mortally wounded by a mortar shell. By his heroic tenacity, at the price of his life, Private Towle saved the lives of many of his comrades and was directly instrumental in breaking up the enemy counterattack.

Leonard A. Funk, Jr.

Rank and organization: first sergeant, U.S. Army, Company C, 508th Parachute Infantry, 82nd Airborne Division. Place and date: Holzheim, Belgium, 29 January 1945. Entered service at Wilkinsburg, Pennsylvania. Birth: Braddock Township, Pennsylvania. G.O. No. 75, 5 September 1945. Citation: 1st Sgt. Leonard A. Funk, Jr., distinguished himself by gallant, intrepid actions against the enemy. After advancing fifteen miles in a driving snowstorm, the American force prepared to attack through waist-deep drifts. The company executive officer became a casualty, and First Sergeant Funk immediately assumed his duties, forming headquarters soldiers into a combat unit for an assault in the face of direct artillery shelling and harassing fire from the right flank. Under his skillful and courageous leadership, this miscellaneous group and the 3rd Platoon attacked fifteen houses, cleared them, and took thirty prisoners without suffering a casualty. The fierce drive of Company C quickly overran Holzheim, netting some eighty prisoners, who were placed under a four-man guard—all that could be spared—while the rest of the understrength unit went about mopping up isolated points of resistance. An enemy patrol, by means of a ruse, succeeded in capturing the guards and freeing the prisoners. The patrol had begun preparations to attack Company C from the rear when First Sergeant Funk walked around the building and into their midst. He was ordered to surrender by a German officer who pushed a machine pistol into his stomach. Although overwhelmingly outnumbered and facing almost certain death, First Sergeant Funk, pretending to comply with the order, began slowly to unsling his submachine gun from his shoulder and then, with a lightning motion, brought the muzzle into line and riddled the German officer. First Sergeant Funk turned on the other Germans, firing and shouting to the other Americans to seize the enemy's weapons. In the ensuing fight, twenty-one Germans were killed, many were wounded, and the remainder were captured. First Sergeant Funk's bold action and heroic disregard for his own safety were directly responsible for the recapture of a vastly superior enemy force, which, if allowed to remain free, could have taken the widespread units of Company C by surprise and endangered the entire attack plan.

* indicates a posthumous award

A paratrooper prepares to engage the enemy with a Dragon antitank rocket. The observer is also armed with two M72 light antiarmor weapons (LAAWs). Both weapons were employed to help destroy Soviet-built BTR-60 armored personnel carriers in use with enemy forces. Note that the observer is also carrying a claymore antipersonnel mine. *82nd Airborne Division War Memorial Museum, Fort Bragg, North Carolina*

continued from page 11

Murphy's Law of Combat, "No plan survives the initial contact." For numerous reasons the paratroopers ended up scattered all over the French countryside. More than half of the glider forces assigned to the 82nd never reached their intended landing zones. The airborne troops would accomplish their mission, and no ground was ever surrendered back to the Germans. However, this came at a very high price: Thirty-three days of fierce fighting left the division with 5,245 paratroopers killed, wounded, or missing.

After the Normandy invasion, the 17th, 82nd, and 101st airborne divisions became part of the XVIII Air borne Corps. The 504th Parachute Infantry Regiment was back up to strength and rejoined the 82nd, and the 507th was reassigned to the 17th Airborne Division.

In September 1944, the 82nd was again in the air as part of Operation Market Garden, in Holland. The operation utilized the three airborne divisions; their mission was to capture and hold critical bridges and

Portrait of a paratrooper during Operation Just Cause, the U.S. invasion of Panama in 1989. During the operation, the soldiers of the 82nd participated in the largest combat jump since World War II. This paratrooper, serving as the radiotelephone operator (RTO), has affixed strips of burlap onto his Kevlar helmet as camouflage. *82nd Airborne Division War Memorial Museum, Fort Bragg, North Carolina*

An M551 Sheridan armored reconnaissance airborne assault vehicle, with all its armament, is shown here during its service in Operation Desert Shield. The M551 featured a 152mm M81 gun/missile launcher, which was capable of firing either an MGM-51 Shillelagh missile or conventional rounds. The vehicle was air-droppable and was used in recon and infantry support to the paratroopers. It was also armed with M240 7.62mm and M2 .50-caliber machine guns. *82nd Airborne Division War Memorial Museum, Fort Bragg, North Carolina*

roads well behind the enemy lines. For the paratroopers of the 82nd, this would be their fourth combat jump. In retrospect the overall operation was deemed overly aggressive; Allied units were defeated at Arnhem. Despite the failure of the operation, the paratroopers of the 82nd carried out their mission and captured the objectives in Graves and Nijmegen. At the end of the operation, the 82nd headed back to France.

In December 1944 the Germans undertook an ambitious operation by mounting an assault in the Ardennes Forest.

Aided by inclement weather and lightning speed, the enemy broke through the lines and caught the Allies totally by surprise. On 18 December the 82nd joined in the battle, thwarting the penetration of the Americans' northern positions by General Von Runstedt's forces.

At the end of the war in Europe, the 82nd Airborne Division was sent to Berlin to serve as an occupation force. During this time, Gen. George Patton had the opportunity to observe the honor guard of the 82nd; he commented, "[Of] all the honor guards I have ever seen, the 82nd's honor guard is

At the onset of Desert Shield, the 82nd Airborne Division was the only force standing between Saddam Hussein's army and Saudi Arabia. The paratroopers stood their ground against what was, at the time, the fourth-largest army in the world. Here a group of paratroopers practices urban combat as they run live-fire exercises in a shooting house. *82nd Airborne Division War Memorial Museum, Fort Bragg, North Carolina*

undoubtedly the best." From that time on, the 82nd Airborne Division became known as "America's Guard of Honor." In January 1946, the 82nd returned stateside to its permanent post at Fort Bragg, North Carolina. There, on 15 November 1948, it was designated as a regular army division.

Post–World War II

After World War II, the 82nd was considered a strategic force in reserve in the event of an armed conflict with the Soviet Union. For this reason the division did not deploy to the Far East during the Korean War. During this time the paratroopers conducted extensive training exercises in every conceivable climate, including arctic, jungle, and desert environments.

Then peacetime training came to an end. In January 1968 the 3rd Brigade of the 82nd Airborne was deployed to the Republic of Vietnam. Here the division fought in engagements in the Mekong Delta and the Iron Triangle and on the Cambodian border. After almost two years in country, the paratroopers of the 3rd Brigade rotated back to Fort Bragg.

After returning home from Vietnam, the division was placed on alert several times during the 1970s. The first time came during the Yom Kippur War in the Middle

Paratroopers of the 82nd Airborne Division examine an Iraqi Mi-24 Hind armed attack helicopter during Desert Storm. The captured helicopter sits on the airfield at the XVIII Airborne Corps base of operations at Rahfa Airport. *82nd Airborne Division War Memorial Museum, Fort Bragg, North Carolina*

East when Egypt and Syria attacked Israel the 82nd and again with the invasion of Zaire. Finally, in 1979 when the American Embassy in Teheran, Iran, was attacked and the Americans were held hostage, the 82nd was poised for a possible rescue mission into Iran.

In October 1983 elements of the 82nd Airborne Division participated in the American invasion on the island of Grenada in the Caribbean. Operation Urgent Fury was the first major military offensive since the Vietnam War. Another mission to Central America came in December 1989, when the 82nd participated in the early hours of Operation Just Cause, the invasion of Panama. This was the first time since World War II that the division conducted a combat jump as they parachuted on Torrijos International Airport in Panama. Following a night combat jump, the paratroopers carried out a follow-on mission in Panama City and the immediate area.

Any celebrating of victory in Panama was short lived; seven months later the 82nd was again placed on

alert and headed off to war. In August 1990 Saddam Hussein's army launched an invasion on the neighboring country of Kuwait. The paratroopers were the leading unit as the largest deployment of U.S. troops began. It was staged in Saudi Arabia, and the 82nd—as part of Desert Shield—was the first line of defense in keeping the Iraqis out of that country.

In January 1991 Desert Shield became Desert Storm when U.S. Special Operations Forces and army attack helicopters opened a passageway into Iraq. Through this air corridor, Allied aircraft pressed their attacks on Iraqi positions, establishing air supremacy early in the war. Six weeks later the ground war began, and the paratroopers of the 82nd took up their place on the flank of the XVIII Airborne Corps. The ground war of Operation Desert Storm would last one hundred hours as U.S. and coalition forces crushed Iraq's military machine. It was yet another victory and battle banner for the 82nd Airborne Division.

Gotcha—another successful operation for the All American Division! A product of the hundred-hour war, an Iraqi prisoner of war is secured by American soldiers. The paratroopers are armed with M16 assault rifles. *82nd Airborne Division War Memorial Museum, Fort Bragg, North Carolina*

Chapter 2

ORGANIZATION

Paratroopers from the 82nd Airborne Division's 1st Brigade Combat Team pass in formation as they prepare to come under new command. *Spc. Jamie Avila*

The 82nd Airborne Division was the first airborne division to be activated during World War II. The division remains the only active airborne division within the U.S. Army, with the 101st Airborne Division having been redesignated an air assault division. Located at Fort Bragg, North Carolina, the 82nd Airborne Division has a strength of nearly fifteen thousand paratroopers. Among these soldiers are more than a thousand jumpmasters and more than five hundred Ranger-qualified soldiers. The following is the stated mission of the 82nd Airborne Division: "Within eighteen hours of notification, the 82nd Airborne Division strategically deploys, conducts forcible entry parachute assault, and secures key objectives for follow-on military operations in support of U.S. national interests."

82nd Airborne Division Units

The division is organized into six brigades and one special battalion. The 1st Brigade Combat Team (1BCT) consists of the 1st Battalion, 504th Parachute Infantry Regiment (the 504th earned the nickname Devils in Baggy Pants during World War II); the 2nd Battalion, 504th Parachute Infantry Regiment; the 4th Squadron, 73rd Cavalry Regiment; the 3rd Squadron, 319th Airborne Field Artillery Regiment; the 307th Brigade Support Battalion; and the 1st Brigade Combat Team, Special Troops Battalion.

Although the airborne divisions of the U.S. Army were not formed until 1942, the concept of the paratrooper dates back to 1784. The idea of sky soldiers has been linked to one of the founding fathers; Benjamin Franklin envisioned

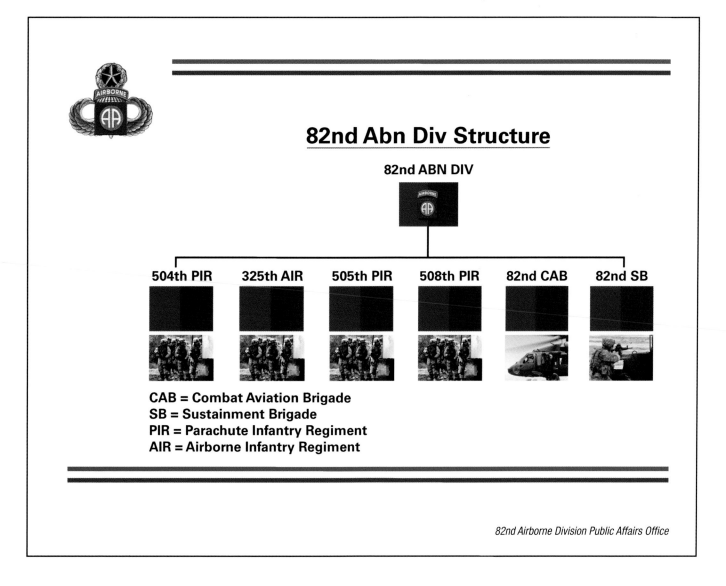

82nd Abn Div Structure

82nd ABN DIV

| 504th PIR | 325th AIR | 505th PIR | 508th PIR | 82nd CAB | 82nd SB |

CAB = Combat Aviation Brigade
SB = Sustainment Brigade
PIR = Parachute Infantry Regiment
AIR = Airborne Infantry Regiment

82nd Airborne Division Public Affairs Office

Paratroopers from Company B, 1st Battalion, 325th Airborne Infantry Regiment, 2nd Brigade Combat Team, bound from building to building while counterattacking an ambush during training on Camp Taji, north of Baghdad. *Sgt. Michael Pryor*

the capability of parachutists in combat. He was clearly a man ahead of his time. Airborne forces descending upon the enemy from above would not become a reality for another 158 years. When the idea did become reality, it was an unstoppable power. For more than sixty-five years the paratroopers have been a vanguard of democracy. Vertical envelopment has been instrumental in bringing down evil regimes from Nazi Germany to the Taliban.

No other military unit can respond more rapidly and effectively to a conflict anywhere in the world than the 82nd Airborne Division (ABD). The 82nd ABD is recognized around the globe as one of the most powerful forces in America's military arsenal. The 504th Parachute Infantry Regiment (PIR) is one of the three infantry regiments of the 82nd and has served as such for more than fifty years.

The 504th PIR was activated on 1 May 1942 at Fort Benning, Georgia. Later that year the U.S. War Department announced plans to form an airborne division. The 82nd Infantry Division, under the command of Maj. Gen. Omar Bradley, was selected as the first American division

to wear the Airborne tab and include the term "Airborne" in its official unit designation. Subsequently, the 504th Parachute Infantry became the first parachute infantry regiment in the newly designated 82nd Airborne Division. Relative to other units in the U.S. Army, however, the 504th is young. Nevertheless, few units are more highly decorated or have a prouder heritage than the Devils in Baggy Pants of the 504th PIR.

On 26 April 1965 the 82nd Airborne Division received orders to prepare to deploy forces to the Caribbean. A revolution had erupted in the Dominican Republic, putting the safety of almost three thousand American citizens in jeopardy. The initial deployment of 82nd Airborne paratroopers came on 30 April. The 504th followed on 3 May, landing at San Isidro Airfield to perform military and humanitarian missions in support of Operation Power Pack. The 504th PIR conducted military operations to help establish and maintain control of Santo Domingo and to provide security along the All American Expressway, which ran through the city.

During this time, the 504th was subject to sniper fire and repeated contact with enemy factions. In spite of these hostile actions, it contributed to the establishment of security and to the distribution of food and medical supplies. Shortly after the arrival of the first U.S. forces, approximately twenty-seven hundred American citizens and fourteen hundred civilians from various nations were evacuated without incident. It became evident that restoring stability to the Dominican Republic required a continued U.S. presence.

The 504th remained part of the Inter-American Peace Force for more than a year, returning to Fort Bragg in the summer of 1966.

Operation Golden Pheasant, Honduras, 1988

In March 1988 the 1st and 2nd battalions of the 504th Parachute Infantry Regiment were joined by soldiers from the 7th Infantry Division at Fort Ord, California, in a deployment to Honduras as part of Operation Golden Pheasant. The deployment had been ordered by President Ronald Reagan in response to actions by the Cuban and Soviet-supported Nicaraguan Sandinistas, who were threatening the stability of the democratic government of Honduras. On 17 March the 1st Battalion landed at Palmerola Airfield, a Honduran air force base that was the headquarters for the U.S. military presence in Honduras. A day later the 2nd Battalion jumped onto the airfield, and the troopers of the 504th began rigorous training exercises with orders to avoid the fighting on the border. In the event that those orders changed, the paratroopers were prepared to engage the Sandinista forces. In only a few days, the Sandinistan government negotiated a truce with enemy leaders, and by the end of March the paratroopers of the 504th had returned home to Fort Bragg.

Operation Just Cause, Panama, 1989

On 20 December 1989 the 504th Parachute Infantry Regiment was again sent into battle as part of Operation Just Cause. The intent of this operation was to protect U.S. civilians in Panama, secure key facilities, neutralize the PDF and the "Dignity Battalions," and restore the elected government of Panama by ousting Gen. Manuel Noriega. The 3rd Battalion had been pre-positioned at Fort Sherman two weeks prior to the operation and was under the control of the 7th Infantry Division.

The battalion conducted air and sea assaults in northern and central Panama to seize the dam controlling the water in the Panama Canal, as well as a prison, several police stations, several key bridges, a PDF supply point, the PDF demolitions school, and an intelligence training facility. The operations were designed to neutralize the PDF while protecting U.S. nationals and the canal itself during the first few hours of the battle.

The 1st and 2nd battalions of the 504th, along with the 4th Battalion of the 325th Airborne Infantry Regiment and the 1st Battalion of the 75th Ranger Regiment, conducted a parachute assault on the Omar Torrijos International Airport. Following the airborne assault, the paratroopers soon found themselves engaged in fierce combat in urban and rural areas. As a testament to the discipline of the soldiers, however, the unit achieved all key objectives while causing only minimal collateral damage.

Desert Storm, 1990

On 2 August 1990 the Iraqi Army attacked and invaded Kuwait. The paratroopers of the 82nd Airborne Division were immediately activated to the defense of Saudi Arabia and were positioned against the enemy, an operation known as Desert Shield. At the time, the Iraqi Army was the fourth-largest army in the world and thus greatly outnumbered the American paratroopers. As diplomatic efforts failed, it became clear that the Iraqi Army was not going to withdraw its forces. Plans were developed for the liberation of Kuwait, and Desert Shield would evolve into Desert Storm.

President George H. W. Bush's warning to Iraqi president Saddam Hussein to withdraw from Kuwait by 15 January 1991 went unheeded. The deadline passed, and the air war began on 17 January. Allied sorties pounded the enemy for more than a month as the XVIII Airborne Corps made a rapid movement westward to position its units to roll up the flank of the Iraqi defense. In a powerful offensive lasting only one hundred hours, the Allied and coalition forces—with the 82nd on the far western flank—crossed into Iraqi territory, overwhelmed the Iraqi Army, and captured thousands of enemy soldiers. The dangerous task of clearing countless enemy bunkers was promptly completed by the 82nd soldiers, and the 504th Parachute Infantry Regiment returned to Fort Bragg in April 1991.

Operation Uphold Democracy, Haiti, 1994

Demonstrating its readiness again in September 1994, the 504th Parachute Infantry Regiment was called upon to take part in Operation Uphold Democracy, intended to be the largest airborne invasion in history. As the main effort of the 82nd Airborne Division, the 504th—along with the 2nd Battalion of the 325th Airborne Infantry Regiment—was tasked to conduct an airborne assault to seize Port-au-Prince International Airport and secure key objectives in Port-au-Prince and the surrounding area to oust Haiti's military dictator Gen. Raul Cedras.

Several months of demanding training had been conducted prior to the invasion to ensure the success of the mission. Last-minute negotiations and knowledge that paratroopers of the 82nd Airborne were en route proved to be the decisive factors in the Haitian dictator's decision to submit to United Nations' directives, and in the U.S. resolve to restore the duly-elected government to power. Less than three hours from drop time, the mission was terminated, and the aircraft returned with the 82nd units to Pope Air Force Base.

Today the 504th Parachute Infantry Regiment stands ready to deploy anywhere in the world within eighteen hours, fully prepared to fight and win. The regiment remains a vital element of America's Guard of Honor and continues to uphold the standards and traditions that have made the Devils in Baggy Pants one of the most prestigious and deadly fighting forces in American military history.

The 2nd Brigade Combat Team, the Falcon Brigade, was made up of the 1st Battalion, 325th Airborne Infantry Regiment "Red Falcons." The 1/325 traces its lineage to the 325th Infantry Regiment, which was activated officially as part of the 82nd Infantry Division on 5 August 1917 at Camp Gordon as part of the All American Division. Other units that trace their lineage back to the 325th Infantry Regiment include the 2nd Battalion, 325th Airborne Infantry Regiment "White Falcons"; the 1st Battalion, 73rd Cavalry Regiment "Blue Falcons"; the 2nd Squadron,

82nd Airborne Patch and Crest

The 82nd Airborne patch is a red square that sits in a blue circle with the letters AA in white. Worn above the patch is a blue tab with the word "AIRBORNE" in white. The symbolism of the patch is depicted by the double "A," referring to the nickname "All American" Division, adopted by the organization in France during World War I. The insignia was approved for the 82nd Division by the adjutant general, American Expeditionary Forces, on 21 October 1918 and was confirmed by the adjutant general, War Department, on 8 July 1922. The insignia was redesignated for the 82nd Airborne Division, and an "Airborne" tab was authorized on 31 August 1942. Authorization for the tab was rescinded on 16 October 1946 but subsequently restored on 23 December 1948 and announced on 1 March 1949.

The unit crest is a silver-colored metal and enamel device consisting of pair of blue enamel stylized wings, tips down, surmounted by a white enamel fleur-de-lis supported by a blue enamel scroll inscribed "In Air, On Land" in silver-colored metal letters. The fleur-de-lis is representative of the battle honors earned in France during World War I. The wings are symbolic of the division's mission. The motto is expressive of the personnel of the organization either on land or in the air.

The distinctive unit insignia was approved on 23 October 1942. It was canceled, and a distinctive unit insignia of the same design as the shoulder sleeve was authorized on 31 July 1990. The original distinctive unit insignia was reinstated on 21 May 1998.

Sgt. Michael Pryor

Fred J. Pushies

319th Airborne Field Artillery Regiment "Black Falcons"; the 407th Brigade Support Battalion "Gold Falcons"; and the 2nd Brigade Combat Team, Special Troops Battalion "Green Falcons."

On 1 May 1965 the 325th deployed to the Dominican Republic as part of Operation Power Pack. Sent with the mission of relieving marines and evacuating civilians, the 325th Airborne Infantry Regiment maneuvered from the airfield at San Isidro into the capital city of Santo Domingo. As the paratroopers advanced through the country, they neutralized communist-backed rebel forces. By the end of May, all rebel resistance had collapsed, and the regiment began peacekeeping and civil affairs operations.

On 26 October 1983 as part of Operation Urgent Fury, the 325th Airborne Infantry Regiment was called on again to spearhead the All American Division's assault on the communist-dominated island of Grenada. Landing at Point Salines Airfield, the 2nd and 3rd battalions, in conjunction with other U.S. forces, overwhelmed the enemy resistance within three days. In addition to defeating the communist forces, U.S. forces rescued 138 students from St. George's Medical University.

During this operation, Bravo Company, 2nd Battalion, was given the mission to assault an area known as Little Havana. The commander of Bravo Company, Capt. Michael Ritz, decided to conduct a recon prior to the assault. At 0430 on 26 October, Captain Ritz and his recon patrol were ambushed. Captain Ritz was killed, but the rest of his patrol, although wounded, survived. Bravo Company soon discovered large caches of weapons and equipment. A squad leader, Staff Sgt. Gary Epps, found a loaded recoilless rifle and decided for the sake of safety to remove the round. The round exploded as he was removing it; he was killed in the explosion.

During Operation Just Cause in December 1989, the 4th Battalion Gold Falcons were attached to the 1st Brigade. The paratroopers conducted a night parachute assault onto Torrijos International Airport, in the Republic of Panama. The Gold Falcons' assault on critical objectives assisted U.S. forces in reestablishing the legitimate democratic government in Panama. This operation was the first combat parachute assault for the 82nd Airborne Division since World War II. The battalion was to jump, assemble,

Capt. Dennis Marshall (center), commander, Company D, 2nd Battalion, 325th Airborne Infantry Regiment, briefs Brig. Gen. John F. Campbell, Multi-National Division-Baghdad deputy commanding general for maneuver, on the progress of construction at the Sadr City Joint Security Station, as Col. Don Farris, commander, 2nd Brigade Combat Team, observes. *Spc. Leigh Campbell*

and perform a helicopter assault on Fort Cimarron to secure the garrison. While this was taking place, Delta Company was tasked to stay behind and secure another airport within Panama City. During that operation, on 21 December, Private James A. Taber Jr. was struck by a sniper's bullet and was killed.

In August 1990 the 325th Airborne Infantry Regiment was called on to spearhead the deployment of U.S. forces to the Persian Gulf in response to the Iraqi invasion of Kuwait.

In a speech on 8 August, President George H. W. Bush told the nation, "A line in the sand has been drawn," and the first U.S. forces were deployed to the Middle East. Among those initial forces was the 82nd Airborne Division's Ready Brigade, the 325th Airborne Infantry Regiment. Its mission was to secure Dahran International Airport and the port of Al Jubayl, Saudi Arabia. These locations would serve as a staging area for the buildup of follow-on U.S. forces. While reinforcements streamed into the country, the 325th, along with the remainder of the 82nd Airborne Division, conducted the most intensive combat training and preparation in the unit's history.

In mid-January after the air war had begun, the 82nd Airborne Division displaced nearly 650 miles to the northwest near the Iraqi border to prepare for the

Sparks fly as Cpl. Benjamin Meyer, a combat engineer with Company A, 325th Special Troops Battalion, 2nd Brigade Combat Team, uses a power saw to cut away storefront locks during an early-morning raid on suspected sniper positions in Baghdad's Adhamiyah district. *Sgt. Michael Pryor*

commencement of the ground war. On 22 February elements of the division, along with soldiers of the 6th French Light Armored Division, began their drive into Iraq. Division soldiers were responsible for the capture of several thousand Iraqi soldiers and the destruction of massive amounts of enemy weapons, equipment, and ammunition. The division is credited with playing a major role in the highly successful one-hundred-hour ground war. The first division elements began redeploying to Fort Bragg on 7 March, and by early April the redeployment of the division was complete.

Currently the 325th Airborne Infantry Regiment has three battalions headquartered at Fort Bragg. The 1st, 2nd, and 3rd battalions comprise the 2nd Brigade of the 82nd Airborne Division.

The 3rd Brigade Combat Team includes the 1/505 Parachute Infantry Regiment, nicknamed the "Panthers"; the 2/505 Parachute Infantry Regiment; the 5/73 Cavalry Regiment; the 1/319 Airborne Field Artillery Regiment; the 82nd Brigade Support Battalion; and the 3BCT Special Troops Battalion.

After World War II, the 505th Parachute Infantry Regiment returned to Fort Bragg. In June 1957 the regiment was reorganized and redesignated as the 505th Infantry and relieved from assignment to the 82nd Airborne Division.

On 25 May 1964 the 505th Infantry was reassigned and redesignated as the 3rd Brigade, 82nd Airborne Division. The brigade was organized into three battalions: the 1/505, 2/505, and 1/508.

On 30 April 1965 the 3rd Brigade was alerted for combat as part of Operation Power Pack, the defense of the Dominican Republic against communist insurgents. Within eighteen hours, the first C-130 landed at San Isidro Airfield, Dominican Republic. After two months of bitter fighting, the 3rd Brigade returned to Fort Bragg. On 24 July 1967 the 3rd Brigade deployed to Detroit, Michigan, to assist local authorities in quelling a civil disturbance. Less than a year later, on 12 February 1968, the 3rd Brigade was alerted for deployment to the Republic of Vietnam in response to the Tet Offensive. In twenty-two months the brigade helped secure the region south of the demilitarized zone (DMZ); it redeployed to Fort Bragg in December 1969. It was the only brigade of the 82nd Airborne Division to participate in the Vietnam conflict.

The 3rd Brigade deployed to Washington, D.C., in May 1971 to help local and federal officials keep demonstrators from disrupting the daily operation of the government. Nine years later, in August 1980, the 1st Battalion (Airborne), 505th Infantry, was alerted and deployed to conduct civil disturbance duty at Fort Indian Gap,

Pennsylvania, during the Cuban refugee internment. The 3rd Brigade deployed the 1st Battalion (Airborne), 505th Infantry, to the Middle East in March 1982 as the first United States member of the Multinational Force & Observers (MFO) rotation in the Sinai Peninsula. The 1/505 returned home in August 1982 from the most important peacekeeping mission in history.

In October 1983 the 3rd Brigade deployed to the country of Grenada to evacuate U.S. citizens and restore free government during Operation Urgent Fury. The brigade remained in Grenada for the duration of the campaign, serving first in combat, then in peacekeeping operations until December 1983. On 3 October 1986 the 505th Parachute Infantry Regiment (PIR) was reactivated under the auspices of the 3rd Brigade with the 1st and 2nd battalions, 505th Parachute Infantry Regiment, and the 1st Battalion, 508th Parachute Infantry Regiment, redesignated as the 3rd Battalion, 505th Parachute Infantry Regiment.

In December 1989 Company A, 3rd Battalion, 505th Parachute Infantry Regiment, participated in Operation Just Cause and assisted in freeing the country of Panama from its dictator, Gen. Manuel Noriega. The efforts assisted Panama in pursuing democracy.

In August 1990 the 505th Parachute Infantry Regiment was airlifted to Saudi Arabia as part of Operation Desert Shield. The ground phase of Operation Desert Storm, which began on 25 February 1991, saw the brigade move north to conduct combat operations through the Euphrates River Valley. After eight months, the brigade had helped secure U.S. objectives; it redeployed to Fort Bragg in April 1991.

In March 1994 the 505th PIR was tasked to organize, train, certify, and deploy a task force made up of National Guard, army reserve, and active-duty troops to serve as part of the Multinational Force and Observers in the Sinai Peninsula. Task Force 4/505, activated on 4 November 1994, was made up of 88 percent National Guard and reservists from thirty-two states, as well as 12 percent active-duty soldiers. The 4/505 deployed to the Sinai from January 1995 through July 1995. On 15 July 1995 the battalion was deactivated.

In September 1994 as part of Operation Restore Democracy, the 505th PIR, along with the rest of the 82nd Airborne Division, was placed on alert. The 505th was scheduled to make combat parachute jumps to help oust the military-led dictatorship and restore the democratically elected president. The 82nd's first wave was in the air, with the 505th loaded onto aircraft awaiting takeoff, when the Haitian military dictators, upon learning that the 82nd was on the way, agreed to step down and avert the invasions.

In December 1994 the 505th PIR participated in Operation Restore Hope. The 2nd Battalion, 505th PIR, departed Fort Bragg for Panama to restore order against the upsurge of Cuban refugees. The battalion participated in safeguarding the Cuban refugees and in actively patrolling in and around the refugee camps.

From July 2002 to January 2003, the 505th PIR deployed to Afghanistan for Operation Enduring Freedom. As part of the multinational force, the 505th engaged in combat operations against al Qaeda and Taliban forces and trained troops for a new Afghan National Army.

From August 2003 to April 2004, the 505th PIR again deployed as part of Operation Iraqi Freedom. The paratroopers trained elements of the Iraqi police, the Facilities Protection Service, the Iraqi Civil Defense Corps, and the new Iraqi army.

The 4th Brigade Combat Team consists of the 1/508 PIR (formerly 3/504) "1-Fury"; the 2/508 Parachute Infantry Regiment (formerly 3/325); the 4/73 Cavalry Regiment; the 2/321 Airborne Field Artillery Regiment; the 782nd Brigade Support Battalion; and the 4BCT Special Troops Battalion.

After the victory in World War II, the 508th returned home from Europe on 24 November 1946, to Camp Kilmer, New Jersey, where the unit was deactivated. A company was reactivated in April 1951; by 1964 the 1st Battalion had been re-formed and reactivated. On 20 April 1965 the Red Devils received a mission to restore peace and provide security to the Dominican Republic under Operation Power Pack. Despite slow progress and bitter fighting, the paratroopers succeeded; they returned home to the United States in July.

With the outbreak of the Tet Offensive, the 508th was on the move again. On 15 February 1968, led by Col. Alexander Bolling, the regiment began arriving in the Republic of Vietnam. The Red Devils played major roles in Operation Yorktown Victor and many others. The

Spc. Jonathan Boynton, a Mk 19 gunner in 3rd Platoon, Troop Bravo, 4th Squadron, 73rd Cavalry Regiment, 4th Brigade Combat Team, investigates a moving object while on patrol in Paktika province, Afghanistan. *Pfc. Micah Clare*

paratroopers served in Vietnam for more than twenty-two months and lost 212 soldiers during the war.

On 25 October 1983 U.S. Army Rangers jumped into Grenada to rescue American medical students. By the morning of 27 October, the Red Devils arrived to take part in Operation Urgent Fury. Within days, the People's Republican Army had surrendered and Cuban Soviet personnel on the island were expelled. The 1/508 remained as a peacekeeping force; it returned on 11 November 1983 to Fort Bragg.

The Red Devils deployed again in January 1985 as part of a multinational observer force in the Sinai Desert. In accordance with the Camp David Treaty, the battalion served for six months as part of an eleven-nation force. Following its tour in the Sinai, the battalion was deactivated at Fort Bragg and relieved from assignment to the 82nd Airborne Division.

On 10 July 1987 the 1/508 was withdrawn from the Combat Arms Regimental System and became part of the 193rd Infantry Brigade (Light) in the Republic of Panama under the U.S. Army Regimental System. The 193rd Infantry had reorganized on 4 December 1986, with a reaffiliation of its two infantry battalions and a field artillery battalion. As a result, the 187th Infantry became the 1/508 Infantry regimentally affiliated with Fort Bragg.

At 1600 on 20 December 1989, the battalion received the executive order to put Operation Just Cause into effect.

The battalion commander ordered the front gate of Fort Amador, Panama, shut down. On 21 December 1989 the 1/508, known as Task Force Devil, cleared the Amador Yacht Club, the Amador Marina, and the La Boca and Balboa housing areas. The Headquarters/Headquarters Company (HHC) continued to patrol the housing area while Alpha and Bravo companies moved back to Amador to secure Panamanian defense buildings. As the soldiers were doing this, the scouts and TOW company secured the front gate of Fort Amador.

Charlie Company 1/508 was tasked with the mission to secure the Comandancia, the headquarters for the Panamanian Defense Forces (PDF) in Panama City. As C Company approached its objective, it came under a hail of sniper fire from the high-rise buildings in the area. The company called for indirect fire on the buildings and breached a hole in the wall of the PDF compound with a forty-pound crater charge. After the company suffered three KIAs (killed in action) and two WIAs (wounded in action), it offered the Panamanians an opportunity to surrender. Charlie Company then began its assault on the Comandancia and started clearing the area. The company secured fourteen of the fifteen buildings in the Comandancia and provided relief in place with the Rangers on 21 December 1989.

The Red Devils conducted various follow-on missions, including perimeter security at refugee camps, Fort Amador, and the La Boca and Balboa housing areas, and as a quick reaction force for any contingencies, including reconnaissance for possible weapons caches, minefields, and other violations of the cease-fire. The 1/508 returned to duty at Fort Kobbe, Panama, in 1994.

In compliance with provisions of the Panama Canal Treaty of 1977, which mandates U.S. forces to withdraw from Panama by noon of 31 December 1999 and mandates the U.S. Army South's Treaty Implementation Program, the Red Devils officially deactivated on 15 October 1994.

On 17 February 1996 the 1/508 was officially reactivated on the U.S. Army rolls, replacing the 3rd Battalion, 325th Infantry. On 27 April 1996 while training in Grafenwohr, Germany, the passing of the colors from Lt. Col. Curtis Scaparrotti to Lt. Col. Arnold Bray marked the Red Devils' official reactivation in Vicenza, Italy. From 1996 to

2000, while the 1/508 was serving in Vicenza, it took part in many training and real-world missions in surrounding countries, including the United Kingdom, Belgium, France, Spain, Norway, Lithuania, Germany, Slovenia, Hungary, Croatia, Bosnia, Bulgaria, Turkey, Kosovo (a province of Serbia), Albania, Sardinia, Tunisia, Sierra Leone, Liberia, Zaire, Burundi, and Botswana.

The mission of the 82nd Combat Aviation Brigade is to find, fix, and destroy enemy forces using aerial fire and maneuver to concentrate and sustain combat power. The 82nd is made up of the 1/82 Attack Reconnaissance Battalion, the 2/82 Assault Battalion, the 3/82 General Support Aviation Battalion, the 122nd Support Aviation Battalion, and the 1/17 Attack Reconnaissance Squadron.

The 82nd Sustainment Brigade is made up of the Sustainment Brigade Special Troops Battalion. Also directly under the 82nd Airborne Division is the Division Special Troops Battalion.

According to U.S. Army Field Manual 71-100, the airborne division can rapidly deploy anywhere in the world to seize and secure vital objectives. It conducts parachute assaults to capture initial lodgments, execute large-scale tactical raids, secure intermediate staging bases or forward operating bases for ground and air operations, or rescue U.S. nationals besieged overseas. The division also can serve as a strategic or theater reserve as well as reinforcement for forward-presence forces.

The airborne division can assault deep into the enemy's rear areas to secure terrain or interdict enemy supply and withdrawal routes. It can seize and repair airfields to provide a forward operating base and airheads for follow-on air-landed forces. It is capable of all other missions assigned to light infantry divisions.

The airborne division uses its strategic and operational mobility to achieve surprise on the battlefield. Its aircraft range and its instrumentation capability enable the air force to accurately deliver the airborne division into virtually any objective area under almost all weather conditions. All equipment is air transportable; most is air-droppable. All personnel are trained for parachute assaults and airborne operations. Engagements with enemy armored or motorized formations require special consideration. The division does not have sufficient armored protection to defeat heavier

The vehicles of 3rd Platoon, Troop Bravo, 4th Squadron, 73rd Cavalry Regiment, 4th Brigade Combat Team, set out on a patrol near a small village in Paktika province, Afghanistan. *Pfc. Micah Clare*

armored formations at close range. Antitank weapons in the division compensate for, but do not completely offset, this deficit.

This differs from an air assault division in that the air assault division combines strategic deployability with tactical mobility within its area of operations (AO). It attacks the enemy deep, fast, and often over extended distances and terrain obstacles. The airmobile division of the Vietnam era provided the U.S. Army the operational foundation, experience, and tactics for today's air assault operations. Air assault operations have evolved into combat, combat support (CS), and combat service support (CSS) elements (aircraft and troops) deliberately task-organized for tactical operations. Helicopters are completely integrated into ground force operations. Air assault operations generally involve insertions and extractions under hostile conditions, as opposed to mere air movement of troops to and from secure locations around the battlefield. Once deployed on the ground, air assault infantry battalions fight like battalions in other infantry divisions; however, normal task organization of organic aviation results in greater combat power and permits rapid aerial redeployment. The fast tempo of operations over extended ranges enables the division commander to quickly seize and maintain the tactical initiative.

Pvt. Mateusz Ozog, of C Company, 1st Battalion, 325th Airborne Infantry Regiment, preps a Raven, a small unmanned aerial vehicle (UAV), for launch during operators' training at the All American Division's drop zone.
Sgt. Michael Pryor

The aviation brigade is a maneuver force of organic, attached, and supporting army aviation units. They include attack, air assault, reconnaissance, electronic warfare (EW), and general support units. The division and aviation brigade commanders can tailor the brigade for virtually any combat, CS, and CSS operation to accomplish division missions.

The brigade is most effective when its aerial forces concentrate at critical times or places to destroy units and exploit enemy vulnerabilities.

The brigade extends the division capability to simultaneously strike the enemy throughout its depth and from multiple directions. When employing the aviation brigade, the division commander considers the following: Attack helicopters are significantly less effective when employed in direct attacks against enemy forces in prepared defensive positions; aviation units have limited nuclear, biological, and chemical (NBC) decontamination capabilities; adverse weather, such as extreme heat and cold, blowing snow and sand, and heavy rain or fog, may hinder aviation operations (currently, only a portion of the aviation brigade's helicopter assets are fully night capable); aviation units have only a limited ability to task-organize below battalion level; and with proper support or augmentation, the aviation brigade

headquarters is capable of planning for, employing, and controlling a task-organized combined-arms force.

The aviation brigade commander may be required to operate over great distances with his forces spread throughout the division's AO. This makes timely and accurate coordination difficult. Coordination is the aviation brigade staff's most important function.

Echelons above corps (EAC) and corps aviation assets are organized into tailored brigades or regiments. These aviation brigades may augment or support the division. Aviation units in these organizations include attack helicopter and assault helicopter battalions, medium helicopter and theater aviation companies, and command aviation battalions.

The division cavalry squadron performs reconnaissance and security for division operations. This helps the division commander to maneuver his brigades and battalions and attack the enemy at the most critical points. The division cavalry squadron, consisting of ground and air troops, is highly mobile. It is ideally suited for economy of force missions as well as reconnaissance and security missions. But must be properly task-organized, augmented, and supported to perform guard and cover missions.

The squadron provides the division commander with real-time information on the enemy and terrain during

Pfc. Josh Baines (left) and Pvt. Mateusz Ozog, of 1st Battalion, 325th Airborne Infantry Regiment, 2nd Brigade Combat Team, pilot the Raven UAV during operators' training. *Sgt. Michael Pryor*

operations, and performs security operations, providing timely warning and force protection to the division. This preserves combat power and prevents premature deployment of the division; fills gaps between units and establishes physical contact with divisional units and adjacent units; facilitates the division's movement with reconnaissance, establishing contact points and passage points, and coordinates with higher and adjacent headquarters; performs reconnaissance and security operations in the division's rear area; and performs damage control and combat operations in the division's rear area when tasked as, or as part of, a tactical combat force (TCF).

A part of the 82nd Combat Aviation Brigade (CAB) is the cavalry, whose purpose is to perform reconnaissance and provide security in close operations. In doing so, the cavalry facilitates the corps or division commander's ability to

maneuver divisions, brigades, and battalions and to concentrate superior combat power and apply it against the enemy at the decisive time and point. Cavalry clarifies, in part, the fog of battle.

The role of the cavalry is defined in U.S. Army Field Manual 17-95 as an economy of force. The flexible capabilities of the cavalry allow the commander to conserve the combat power of divisions or brigades for engagement where he desires. The combat power of cavalry units, in particular, makes them ideal for offensive and defensive missions as an economy of force.

Cavalry serves as a catalyst that transforms the concepts of maneuver warfare into a battlefield capability. Maneuver is the essence of U.S. fighting doctrine. In the tactical sense, maneuver is the swift movement and positioning of combat forces to attack an enemy's vulnerability, such as flanks,

U.S. Army 82nd Airborne Division soldiers practice loading a casualty into a paratrooper medical platform vehicle during practical combat exercises at the tactical combat casualty care class on Contingency Operating Base Speicher. *Spc. Amanda Morrissey*

rear, lines of communication, service support capability, or isolated elements. Maneuver is the means to seize or retain the initiative, and to create or exploit offensive opportunities. It is also the means to concentrate superior combat power against the enemy at the right time and place. For maneuver to be successful, the commander must have a high degree of situational awareness. He must reduce the enemy, terrain, and friendly unknowns of the battlefield to fight effectively and to operate within the enemy's decision cycle. The successful execution of maneuver warfare continues to be the product of thorough reconnaissance and continual security. As the "eyes and ears" of the commander, cavalry provides the commander with situational awareness and enhances his ability to maneuver successfully.

Cavalry has historically served as a flexible multipurpose force. Capitalizing on a significant mobility advantage over infantry, cavalry performed long-range reconnaissance and security for commanders. These missions gave commanders the ability to maneuver and concentrate forces on a battlefield for decisive battle. Once on the chosen field, cavalry continued to play key roles such as close reconnaissance

to detect enemy weaknesses, close security to protect the flanks or rear of the infantry line, countering enemy cavalry, counterattacking enemy infantry attacks, administering the decisive blow to a faltering enemy, covering retreat, and pursuing a retreating enemy.

Pathfinder—RSTA

From World War II through the cold war, the 82nd Airborne Division utilized soldiers trained in Pathfinder operations. According to Maj. Tom Earnhardt, 82nd Airborne Division, these pathfinder skills have been absorbed into the reconnaissance, surveillance, and target acquisition (RSTA) mission. The doctrine for RSTA support for joint operations defines that the RSTA missions and tasks are used within broad strategic, operational, and tactical areas. Reference mission areas and the manner in which the products are used are not meant to categorize types of systems as strategic, operational, or tactical. Rather they demonstrate RSTA support at the various levels of war and establish the scope of application for the products of those operations. The primary objective of RSTA operations is to support military operations across the operational continuum. RSTA operations are performed by forces with a primary RSTA mission and other forces with either a collateral mission or the capability to perform such a mission.

Modern intelligence collection systems can accumulate vast amounts of information. To be useful, the information must be relevant, accurate, analyzed, properly formatted, and disseminated in a timely manner to the appropriate user. Also, the information must be appropriately classified to protect the RSTA system and its technology but sanitized to the degree necessary to allow dissemination to the appropriate user level.

RSTA mission areas are essentially the same for the strategic, operational, and tactical levels of operations and interest. However, the tasking within these mission areas varies based on the level, focus, need, and forces available. RSTA mission areas include indications and warning (I&W), planning and employment, and assessment. Tactical RSTA operations forces and assets can provide the required detailed information (that is, terrain, enemy disposition, orders of battle, movement, and offensive and defensive capabilities) needed to plan and to employ forces successfully. This support includes providing target detection and acquisition, near-real-time intelligence, and so forth, which provide opportunities for offensive and defensive actions and help reduce casualties and achieve victory.

RSTA operations provide assessment support to all levels of command before, during, and after the conduct of military operations. They can provide an important means for assessing friendly deception efforts. Assessments such as bomb damage assessment (BDA) can provide information on the success of military operations and the need for follow-up or new operations. They can assist in determining where and when to employ scarce resources and concentrate efforts. Such assessments affect the formulation of policy and military plans at all levels of conflict.

UAVs

The 82nd Airborne Division has come into the twenty-first century with the addition of unmanned aerial vehicles (UAV). The 2nd Brigade Combat Team (BCT) of the 82nd Airborne Division is the first brigade in the U.S. Army to field the Raven UAV, a battery-powered UAV that is hand launched by a soldier. The Raven may look like a remote-control toy airplane to the average person, but it's actually a very capable military UAV. The device, used for reconnaissance and surveillance, transmits live video images and information from aloft directly to battlefield commanders on the ground.

The Raven system consists of the UAV and its payload, a ground control station, and a remote video terminal, all of which together weigh less than forty pounds and can be broken down and carried in a rucksack. The Raven flies 150 to one thousand feet above ground level with a range of more than ten kilometers.

Entering service with the paratroopers in 2003, the Raven system, referred to as the Raven A model, has been used with great success in Operation Enduring Freedom and Operation Iraqi Freedom.

Medical Training

A soldier sitting in the rear passenger seat of a Humvee cries out in pain as he reacts to an "injury" caused by an improvised explosive device (IED) in Tikrit, Iraq. The soldier driving the vehicle immediately stops and struggles to reach his comrade. He climbs over the equipment and other gear, reaches over the back seat, and begins working on the wounded soldier, applying a tourniquet to his leg in an attempt to save his life.

As the soldier feverishly works on his teammate, an instructor yells out, "Time's up! Switch partners!" The above incident is not an actual war casualty but rather a training scenario for tactical combat casualty care (TC3) class at the 82nd Airborne Division Troop Medical Clinic on Contingency Operating Base Speicher.

"The TC3 class focuses primarily on preventing the cause of loss of life on the battlefield, which is bleeding," said Staff Sgt. Audrey David, a medic and TC3 instructor with C Company, 82nd Brigade Support Battalion, 3rd Brigade Combat Team, 82nd Airborne Division.

Chapter 3

TRAINING

During the second week of training, known as Tower Week, at the U.S. Army Airborne School, students practice aircraft exit and how to recover immediately after a landing. Here students pull one another to get the feel of being caught by a crosswind upon landing. *JO1 Jim Conner*

Airborne Training

The separation of the paratrooper from his fellow soldiers begins in the hot Georgia sun. Airborne training for the prospective airborne trooper is conducted at the U.S. Army Airborne School, at Fort Benning, Georgia. For the next three weeks, he will be at the mercy of the army's "Black Hats," the airborne instructors of the 1st Battalion (Airborne), 507th Parachute Infantry Regiment, who will convert a "leg" into an "airborne" trooper. He will learn what it takes to hurl himself out of a perfectly good airplane for the purpose of infiltrating into his mission drop zone (DZ), and he will run (a lot).

He will also learn a new mantra, which he will repeat over and over during the three-week course at Fort Benning. He will shout out "Motivated!" three times, then "Airborne!" and then he will run. He will repeat the mantra "Fired up!" three times, then "Airborne!" And when his body is aching and cannot move another inch, he will run some more. These veteran Airborne-qualified instruc-tors wearing the Black Hats ensure that these potential Green Berets are indeed motivated and fired up. This is far more than an evolution. This is Airborne!

Basic airborne training is broken into three weeklong segments: Ground Week, Tower Week, and Jump Week.

During Ground Week, trainees start an intensive program of instruction designed to prepare them to complete a parachute jump. They learn how to execute a flawless parachute landing fall (PLF) to land safely in the landing zone (LZ). The PLF consists of five points of contact designed to absorb the shock of landing and distribute it across the balls of the feet, the calves, the thighs, the buttocks, and the push-up muscles of the back. Practicing on mockups of a C-130 and a C-141, the troopers learn the proper way to exit an aircraft. They climb a thirty-four-foot tower, where they are connected to the lateral drift apparatus (LDA) and, upon command, assume door position, then follow the command to "Jump!" The troopers' proper body position is evaluated, and they must jump over and over again until the Black Hats are happy.

The Airborne Creed

I am an Airborne trooper! A Paratrooper!

I jump by parachute from any plane in flight. I volunteered to do it, knowing well the hazards of my choice.

I serve in a mighty Airborne Force—famed for deeds in war—renowned for readiness in peace. It is my pledge to uphold its honor and prestige in all I am—in all I do.

I am an elite trooper—a sky trooper—a shock trooper—a spearhead trooper. I blaze the way to far-flung goals—behind, before, above the foe's front line.

I know that I may have to fight without support for days on end. Therefore, I keep mind and body always fit to do my part in any Airborne task. I am self-reliant and unafraid. I shoot true, and march fast and far. I fight hard and excel in every art and artifice of war. I never fail a fellow trooper. I cherish as a sacred trust the lives of men with whom I serve. Leaders have my fullest loyalty, and those I lead never find me lacking.

I have pride in the Airborne! I never let it down!

In peace, I do not shirk the dullest of duty; I do not protest the toughest training. My weapons and equipment are always combat ready. I am neat of dress, military in courtesy, proper in conduct and behavior.

In battle, I fear no foe's ability, nor underestimate his prowess, power, and guile. I fight him with all my might and skills—ever alert to evade capture or escape a trap. I never surrender, though I be the last.

My goal in peace or war is to succeed in any mission of the day—or die, if need be, in the try.

I belong to a proud and glorious team—the Airborne, the army, my country. I am its chosen pride to fight where others may not go—to serve them well until the final victory.

I am the trooper of the sky! I am my nation's best! In peace and war I never fail. Anywhere, anytime, in anything—I am Airborne!

Fig. 1

U.S. Army

Parachute landing fall procedures from the U.S. Army Manual for Static Line Parachuting specify that when the balls of your feet make contact with the ground, several actions must occur at the same time (see figure 1). You must place your chin on your chest, tense your neck muscles, bring your elbows high in front of your face, and expose the second and third points of contact (calf and thigh, respectively) by shifting and bending your knees, maintaining pressure with your opposite knee. You must rotate your upper body (from the waist up) around toward the opposite direction of drift. Your body should be contorted in an arc, and you should expose the four remaining points of contact at this time. You should lay the points of contact down on the ground in sequence, then bring your feet up and around your opposite shoulder, completing the fall on your back.

Next comes Tower Week. Now that the trainees have learned how to exit, position, and land, they use this week to refine those skills. In a training device known as the swing landing tower (SLT), they are hooked up to a parachute harness, then they jump from a 12-foot-

Airborne trainees make their jump from the 35-foot tower at Fort Benning, Georgia. During Tower Week the students build confidence as they practice their parachuting skills in preparation for an actual jump. *Capt. Kinal Sztalkoper*

During Tower Week the students practice and refine the exiting, positioning, and landing skills learned during Ground Week. Working out of a 35-foot tower takes the training to the next level. *Capt. Kinal Sztalkoper*

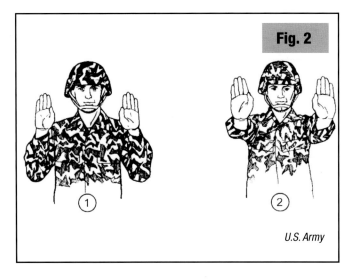

Fig. 2

U.S. Army

Fig. 3

U.S. Army

high elevated platform. The apparatus provides the downward motion and oscillation, simulating that of an actual parachute jump.

To make things more challenging for the students, the instructors have control of the SLT and can determine whether each student should have a hard or a soft landing. As each student rushes toward the ground, hands clinging to the harness, the instructor yells, "Hazard left!" and leans into the rope controlling the drop. He watches as the airborne trainees hit the ground, and they better have landed in a manner to avoid the imaginary obstacle, or the "Airborne sergeant" will have a few choice words for them, and a number of pushups too.

During Week Two, the students get to ride the "Tower." It's designed to give them practice in controlling their parachute during the descent from 250 feet, and execute a PLF upon landing. They also learn how to handle parachute malfunctions. And they will run.

Finally Week Three, Jump Week. The potential paratroopers perform five parachute jumps. First, each trooper jumps with a T-10B chute. Next is a mass exit with equipment and a T-10B chute, then another individual exit with an MC1-1B chute and tactical assembly. The fourth jump is a mass exit at night with a T-10B and tactical equipment. The fifth jump is either an individual jump with an MV1-1B chute or a mass jump with a T-10B chute.

The U.S. Army's Guide for Airborne Students states "Airborne training is a rite of passage for the warrior." Upon graduation, students are awarded the coveted Silver Wings and are qualified as "Airborne" troopers.

Jump Command Sequence and Hand Signals

According to the U.S. Army Manual for Static Line Parachuting Techniques and Training (FM-21), the jumpmaster (JM) gives a sequence of nine jump commands to ensure positive control of the parachutists inside the aircraft and immediately before exiting. Every command requires specific actions by each parachutist. Properly executed commands ensure a safe exit from the aircraft. The commands are given orally, but, as a backup because of aircraft engine noise, arm-and-hand signals are also used with each command.

Get ready is the first jump command. This command alerts the parachutists seated in the aircraft and directs their complete attention to the JM. The JM starts the command with his arms at his sides, then gives the arm-and-hand signal by extending both arms to the front at shoulder level with palms facing the parachutists. He begins at shoulder level, fingers and thumbs extended and joined, palms facing toward the parachutists. He extends both arms forward until the elbows lock, with the palms toward the parachutists. He gives the oral command "get ready," then returns to the start position with arms at the sides.

During Week Two the students get to ride the tower. It's designed to give them practice in controlling their parachute during the descent from 250 feet and executing a PLF upon landing. During this phase of training, the students learn how to handle parachute malfunctions.

Capt. Kinal Sztalkoper

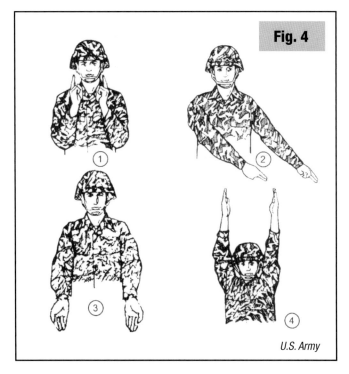

Fig. 4

U.S. Army

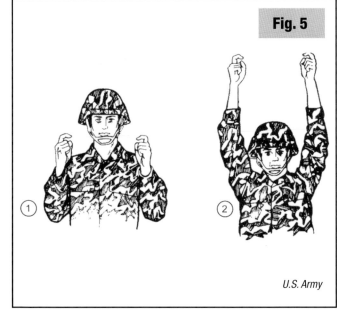

Fig. 5

U.S. Army

"Stand in the door!" The command is given and the students prepare to throw themselves out of a perfectly good airplane. The potential paratroopers perform five parachute jumps during Jump Week. Jumps are made with and without equipment and include a night jump. *Capt. Kinal Sztalkoper*

It is the ultimate thrill ride that no amusement park can duplicate. Once the student reaches the top of the 250-foot tower, he hangs for a moment, then he releases the parachute released and gravity takes over. The tower normally accommodates up to three jumpers at a time, although this can change depending on wind conditions.
Capt. Kinal Sztalkoper

Outboard personnel, *stand up* is the second jump command. For this command, the arm-and-hand signal has two parts. Part One: The JM starts with his hands at the shoulders, index and middle fingers of each hand extended and joined, and the remaining fingers and the thumbs curled to the palms (see figure 2). He gives the command "outboard personnel," lowers his arms down to his sides at a 45-degree angle, and locks his elbows. Part Two: The JM gives the command "stand up." He extends and joins the fingers and thumb of each hand, rotates the hands so the palms face up, then raises his arms straight overhead, keeping his elbows locked (see figure 3). At this command, the parachutists sitting nearest the outboard side of the aircraft stand up, raise and secure the seats, face the jump doors, and assume the shuffle position.

Soldiers perform a static line jump from a C-17 Globemaster III aircraft. During Jump Week the students have to make five parachute jumps to earn their silver jump wings. Only then will they be considered Airborne soldiers. *U.S. Air Force*

U.S. Army

he extends and joins the fingers and thumb of each hand, rotates his hands so the palms face up, and raises his arms straight overhead, keeping the elbows locked. The parachutists seated inboard react in the same manner as the outboard personnel described in the previous paragraph.

Hook up is the fourth jump command (see figure 5). The JM begins with his arms either extended directly overhead with elbows locked or with his arms bent, hands at shoulder level. He forms a hook with the index finger of each hand, and forms a fist with the remaining fingers and thumb of each hand. As he gives the oral command, he moves his arms down and up in a pumping motion. He repeats the arm-and-hand signal at least three times.

At this command, each parachutist detaches the static line snap hook from the top carrying handle of the reserve parachute and hooks up to the appropriate anchor linecable, with the open portion of the snap hook toward the outboard side of the aircraft.

Each parachutist must ensure that the snap hook locks properly. The jumper inserts the safety wire in the hole and folds it down; to protect his eyes, he inserts the wire by pointing it toward the rear of the aircraft. Then the jumper forms a bight in the static line and held at eye level. The bight is not released until the parachutist moves into the door. Personnel jumping out of the left (right) door have the static line over their left (right) shoulder.

Inboard personnel, stand up is the third jump command (see figure 4). As with the outboard signal before, inboard also has two parts. Part One: The JM starts with his hands centered on his chest at shoulder level, index and middle fingers extended and joined, remaining fingers and thumbs curled to the palms. He gives the command "inboard personnel," extends his arms forward at a 45-degree angle, toward the inboard seats, and locks his elbows. Part Two: The JM gives the command "stand up." He first rotates his arms to the sides and down at a 45-degree angle. Then

Jumpers exit a C-130 aircraft en masse as they perform basic airborne training. The students may jump from any of an assortment of aircraft, from C-130 turboprop planes to the newer C-17 Globemaster III jet-powered aircraft.
U.S. Army

Fig. 7

①

②

U.S. Army

The most beautiful sight that a paratrooper will ever see is a full canopy. Here a soldier swings under his parachute after jumping from a C-17 Globemaster III of the 15th Airlift Squadron, Charleston Air Force Base. *Staff Sgt. Jeremy T. Lock, U.S. Air Force*

Check static lines is the fifth jump command (see figure 6). This is a plural command because there are several static lines attached to the anchor line cable. The JM begins the command at eye level, with his thumb and index finger of each hand forming an "O." Then he extends and joins his remaining fingers with palms facing in. As he gives the oral command, he extends his arms to the front until his elbows are nearly locked, then returns to the starting position.

He repeats the arm-and-hand signal at least three times, ensuring that the knife edge of his hands is toward the parachutists and his palms face each other.

Upon receiving this command, each parachutist checks his static line and the static line of the parachutist to his front, checking visually and by feeling with his free hand. He does not release the bight for checks. He verifies the following items: The static line snap hook is properly attached to the anchor line cable with the safety wire properly inserted; the

Fig. 8

U.S. Army

static line is free of frays and tears; the static line is not misrouted and is properly stowed on the pack tray; all excess slack in the static line is taken up and stowed in the static line slack retainer; the pack closing tie is routed through the pack opening loop; and the pack tray is intact.

The last two jumpers in each stick face about. The next to last jumper inspects the last jumper's static line and gives him a sharp tap to indicate that the static line and pack tray have been checked and are safe for jumping. Each parachutist gives the parachutist to his front a sharp tap, signifying that the static line and pack tray have been checked and are safe for jumping.

Check equipment is the sixth jump command (see figure 7). The JM starts this arm-and-hand signal with his fingertips

Soldiers load onto a C-17 for a night jump. *U.S. Air Force*

At this command, each parachutist checks his equipment, starting at the helmet, and ensures that there are no sharp edges on the rim of his ballistic helmet and that the chin strap and parachutist retention straps are properly routed and secured. He then physically seats the activating lever of the chest strap ejector snap and the leg strap ejector snaps. If jumping with combat equipment, he also ensures that the ejector snap of the lowering line is properly attached and seated. He completes these actions with his free hand while maintaining a firm grip on the static line bight with the other hand.

Sound off for equipment check is the seventh jump command (see figure 8). The JM cups his hands and places his thumbs behind his ears. He gives the oral command "sound off for equipment check."

At this command, the last parachutist in the outboard stick sounds off, saying "OK," and gives the parachutist in front a sharp tap on the thigh. The signal is continued until it gets to the Number 1 parachutist, who notifies the JM by pointing to him and saying, "All OK, jumpmaster." For a C-130 aircraft, this signal is passed to the Number 25 parachutist (just forward of the wheel well), who forms a circle with the index

centered on his chest, palms facing the chest, and the fingers and thumb of each hand extended and joined. Or he may instead extend his arms to the sides at shoulder level, fingers and thumbs extended and joined, and palms facing toward the parachutist. He gives the oral command, extends his arms to the sides at shoulder level, then returns them to his chest. Or he may instead bend his arms at the elbows, bringing his fingertips to the center of his chest, then return to the extended position. He repeats the arm-and-hand signal at least three times. (The JM must check his own equipment.)

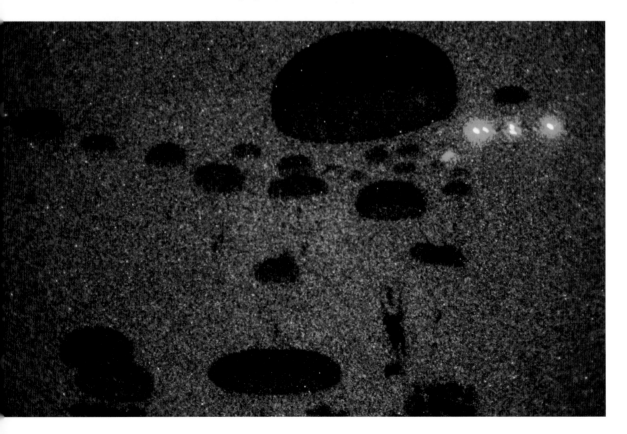

Parachutes fill the night sky as jumpers exit from a C-17 aircraft. A night parachute jump is required for completion of the Basic Airborne School.
Sgt. Michael Pryor

finger and thumb of his free hand, turns toward the center of the aircraft, and gives the OK signal to Number 24 (the last parachutist of the inboard stick). The tap and indication that all previous parachutists are OK is passed up to Number 4, the first parachutist of the inboard stick, who signals Number 3, the first parachutist to the rear of the wheel well. The signal is continued until it gets to the Number 1 parachutist, who notifies the JM by pointing to the JM and saying, "All OK." A parachutist who has an equipment problem notifies the JM, the assistant jumpmaster (AJM), or safety personnel by raising his outboard hand high above the anchor line cable, palm facing the JM. The parachutists do not pass this signal. The JM, the AJM, or safety personnel either correct the deficiency or remove the parachutist from the stick.

Stand by is the eighth jump command (see figure 9). This command is given about ten seconds before the aircraft

---

U.S. Army Parachutist Badge

The first parachutist badge was designed during World War II by Capt. (later Lt. Gen.) William P. Yarborough, of the 501st Parachute Battalion. The parachutist badge was formally approved on 10 March 1941. The senior and master parachutists badges were authorized by Headquarters, Department of the Army, in 1949.

Symbolism

The wings suggest flight and, together with the open parachute, symbolize individual proficiency and parachute qualifications.

Basic Parachutist

Awarded to any individual who has satisfactorily completed the prescribed proficiency tests while assigned or attached to an Airborne unit or the Airborne Department of the Infantry School or has participated in at least one combat parachute jump.

Senior Parachutist

Participated in a minimum of thirty jumps, including fifteen jumps with combat equipment; two night jumps, one of which is as jumpmaster of a stick; two mass tactical jumps that culminate in an airborne assault problem; graduated from the jumpmaster course; and served on jump status with an Airborne unit or other organization authorized parachutists for a total of at least twenty-four months.

Master Parachutist

Participated in sixty-five jumps, including twenty-five jumps with combat equipment; four night jumps, one of which is as

Parachute wings (top to bottom): basic, senior, master, and combat jump. *Fred J. Pushies*

jumpmaster of a stick; five mass tactical jumps that culminate in an airborne assault problem with a unit equivalent to a battalion or larger; separate company/battery or organic staff of regiment size or larger; graduated from the jumpmaster course; and served in jump status with an Airborne unit or other organization that has authorized parachutists for a total of at least thirty-six months.

Combat parachutist badges that have stars representing participation in combat jumps had been worn unofficially on parachute wings during and after World War II. This practice did not gain official sanction until after the 1983 invasion of Grenada, Operation Urgent Fury. Small stars are superimposed on the appropriate badge to indicate combat jumps as follows: one combat jump, a bronze star centered on the shroud lines below the canopy; two combat jumps, a bronze star on the base of each wing; three combat jumps, a bronze star on the base of each wing and one star centered on the shroud lines below the canopy; four combat jumps, two bronze stars on the base of each wing; five combat jumps, a gold star centered on the shroud lines below the canopy.

reaches the release point and only after the aircraft has cleared all obstacles near the drop zone. Starting with his hands up at shoulder level, the JM extends and joins the index and middle fingers of each hand, curling the remaining fingers and the thumb of each hand toward the palm. He extends his arms down to his sides at a 45-degree angle, locks his elbows, and points to both doors at the same time.

At this command, parachutist Number 1 shuffles toward the door, establishes eye contact with the safety, hands the safety his static line, holds his elbows firmly into his sides with his palms on the end of the reserve parachute, turns and centers himself in the open jump door, and awaits the command "go."

Go is the ninth jump command. The green light is the final time warning on U.S. Air Force aircraft. It tells the JM that the aircrew feels that conditions are safe and it is time to issue the ninth jump command. The JM gives the verbal command "go" and may also tap the first parachutist out. In this case, the command "go" and a sharp tap on the thigh is the signal to exit. At the command "go," the first parachutist exits the aircraft. All subsequent jumpers begin moving toward the door using a shuffle. Once the jumpers begin to shuffle, they assume an elbow-locked position with the arm that is controlling their static line. The jumpers place their static line control hand so it is nearly touching the back of the pack tray of the jumper in front of them. This establishes the proper jump interval.

An airborne artilleryman from B Battery, 2nd Battalion, 319th Airborne Field Artillery Regiment, 2nd Brigade Combat Team, parachutes into battle while fellow soldiers prepare to fire a 105mm Howitzer during a heavy drop exercise at Drop Zone (DZ) Sicily. *Sgt. Michael Pryor*

Jumpers do not position their static line control hand so that it extends past the pack tray of the jumper in front of them. As each jumper approaches the door, he establishes eye contact with the safety and hands his static line to him. Once the safety has control of the jumper's static line, the jumper returns his hand to the end of the reserve parachute with his fingers spread. After handing his static line to the safety (in the vicinity of the lead edge of the door), the jumper executes a left or right turn (as appropriate) and faces directly toward and centered on the door, with both hands over the ends of the reserve parachute, fingers spread. He continues the momentum of his movement by walking toward the door, focusing on the horizon, and stepping on the jump platform. He pushes off with either foot and vigorously jumps up and

out, away from the aircraft. He immediately snaps into a good, tight body position and exaggerates the bend into his hips to form an L shape.

Advanced Airborne Training

According to 1st Sgt. Albert Hinton, at the Advanced Airborne School (AAS) located at Fort Bragg, "The Advanced Airborne School was started in 1947; it was then known as the 'Heavy Drop School.' The school operated as a three-day course in which techniques of heavy drop were taught. In 1949 the school closed and opened again in May 1950, this time with the jumpmaster course integrated into the school."

During the jumpmaster course, students are required to learn and test the following to complete the thirteen-day course. The first three days of the course focus on instruc-

2nd Lt. Larry Pitts, the officer in charge of the fire direction center for B Battery, 2nd Battalion, 319th Airborne Field Artillery Regiment, 2nd Brigade Combat Team, maintains communication with forward observers while his team does the calculations to send a fire mission during a heavy drop exercise at DZ Sicily. *Sgt. Michael Pryor*

tional material that encompasses a variety of information. Each student is required to take an examination on the following subjects and maintain a minimal of 70 percent on all examinations. Nomenclature students are required to know every item of equipment located on the T-10 main parachute and the soft loop center pull modified improved reserved parachute system (MIRPS). The student must correctly identify eighteen out of twenty-five random items of equipment, using proper nomenclature, to obtain a minimum score of 70 percent.

During their time at AAS, students participate in pre-jump training, better known as sustained airborne training. In thirty minutes or less, each student must be able to give pre-jump training to an instructor by reciting, verbatim, the titles of the five points of performance, recovery

and turn-in of equipment, malfunctions, activation of the reserve parachute, towed parachutist procedures, entanglements, emergency landings, B-7 life preserver, night jumps, adverse weather aerial delivery system (AWADS) jumps, and parachute landing falls—without failing to discuss any major area. AWADS is the precise delivery of personnel, equipment, and supplies during adverse weather using a self-contained aircraft instrumentation system without artificial ground assistance or the use of ground navigational aids.

Students must also demonstrate all slips and turns and the two methods of recovery from the drag to obtain a minimum score of 70 percent. In a written exam the student must also be able to correctly answer 70 percent of the questions pertaining to all phases of an airborne operation and duties conducted by select personnel that support the mission.

Practical work in the aircraft (PWAC)

Given an S-3 air briefing, sustained airborne training, student station time, an air force aircraft, and a pre-designated drop zone, each student must perform all phases of the duties of the jumpmaster, including locating reference points and safely conducting an airborne operation in accordance with the 82nd Airborne Division. Students must obtain a minimum score of 70 percent.

Jumpmaster personnel inspection (JMPI)

Students must conduct JMPI on three jumpers in a controlled environment, with the three jumpers typically wearing the following equipment: T-10D main parachute and soft loop center pull reserve parachute, ballistic helmet, M1950 weapons case, all-purpose lightweight individual carrying equipment (ALICE) pack rigged with a harness single-point release and a hook pile tape lowering line, rigged to be jumped and lowered as a tandem load. Standard: To pass, each student must inspect all three jumpers utilizing the proper sequence, identifying and calling off any deficiencies they may find using proper nomenclature, within five minutes, to obtain a minimum score of 70 percent.

Air Movement Operations Course

Sgt. 1st Class William Johnson, non-commissioned officer in charge (NCOIC) of the air movement operations (AMO) course, relates: "Many units, when they deploy, move by military air—a high-performance air force aircraft specifically designed to transport cargo and personnel. The air movement operations course is a thirteen-day course designed to teach students, after the deployment order is received, to properly prepare their unit's personnel, equipment, and materials for movement by military air.

After successful completion of the AMO course, students return to their parent unit and can take any cargo designated by their commander, both hazardous and nonhazardous, and prepare and certify it according to federal regulations for military air shipment as secondary cargo, on a 463L pallet or in a freight container.

Students receive hands-on instruction in identifying hazardous materials, certifying them as safe according to the applicable air force manuals, and ensuring that they have been properly prepared for shipment. The students

The All-American Freefall Team is a sport parachute team formed more than twenty-five years ago to represent the famed 82nd Airborne All American Division, Fort Bragg, North Carolina. The team is the official representative of the 82nd and has proudly represented the Airborne division across the United States. *82nd Airborne Division Public Affairs Office*

also practice building 463L pallets and properly securing the cargo load, loading and securing vehicles on aircraft, and weighing and marking vehicles and equipment. Students prepare multiple load plans for all types of air force cargo aircraft and determine how to make maximum effective usage of the aircraft.

The course is divided into three phases. The first week, Phase I, deals with hazardous materials; the second week, Phases II and III, covers equipment preparation and load planning. Students regularly spend time after class completing homework and studying.

All-American Freefall Team

The All-American Freefall Team is a sport parachute team formed more than twenty-five years ago at Fort Bragg to represent the famed 82nd Airborne All American Division. It has members from many units within the division. The team has performed more than six thousand freefall demonstrations. It is the official representative of the 82nd and has proudly represented the division across the United States at military ceremonies and activities, air shows, fairs, competitions, civic functions, and professional and collegiate sports events.

Chapter 4

WEAPONS

The M9 was introduced as the standard-issue sidearm for U.S. troops in 1985. Lt. Col. Al Shoffner (foreground), commander of the 2nd Battalion, 319th Airborne Field Artillery Regiment, 2nd Brigade Combat Team, 82nd Airborne Division, and Lt. Col. Yahyaw Rasol Abdalh, commander of the 3rd Battalion, 2nd Brigade, 6th Iraqi Army Division, engage in a friendly marksmanship competition with their M9 pistols at the firing range on their shared combat outpost in Adhamiyah, Baghdad. *Sgt. Michael Pryor*

M9 Beretta

Since 1985, the M9 has seen service as the standard-issue sidearm for U.S. troops, both conventional and special, in Operation Urgent Fury in Grenada, Operation Desert Shield/Desert Storm in Kuwait, and Operation Restore Hope in Somalia; in service with an implementation force (IFOR) in Bosnia and Kosovo force (KFOR) in Kosovo; and now in global war on terrorism (GWOT) operations. Along with the standardization of the 9mm round, the M9 brought the armed forces a larger-capacity magazine. The M9 holds fifteen rounds compared to the Colt 1911's seven or eight rounds. Although the 9mm ammunition is lighter and smaller, it is viewed as adequate for line troops. This tradeoff also allowed the troops to engage more rounds in a firefight before needing to reload, with an average life of 72,250 rounds. The slide is open for nearly the entire length of the barrel, which facilitates the ejection of spent shells and virtually eliminates stoppages. The open slide configuration also provides a means for the pistol to be loaded manually. Worth noting is the fact that conventional troops in general and U.S. Special Operations Forces (SOF) units in particular have voiced their dislike of the lightweight 9mm round, preferring the heavier .45-caliber ammunition. In light of this, the armed forces are revisiting the current range of .45-caliber sidearms available.

M4A1

Soldiers of the 82nd Airborne Division are currently issued the M4A1 carbine. The M4A1, from Colt Arms of Connecticut, is a smaller, compact version of the full-size M16A2 rifle. The M4A1 weapon was designed specifically for the U.S. Special Operations Forces; however, since its introduction, the weapon has found its way into conventional units. The M4A1 is designed for when speed of action and light weight are required. The primary weapon for U.S. SOF units, it has also become common issue in other elite units among the armed forces. The barrel has been shortened to 14.5 inches, which reduces the weight while maintaining the weapon's effectiveness for quick handling in field operations. The retractable buttstock has intermediate stops, allowing versatility in

The M203 grenade launcher is a lightweight, single-shot, breech-loaded 40mm weapon specifically designed for placement beneath the barrel of the M4A1 carbine. With a quick-release mechanism, the M203 can be added to the M4A1 carbine to create the versatility of a weapon system capable of firing 5.56mm ammunition as well as an expansive range of 40mm high-explosive and special-purpose munitions. Spc. James "Wonger" Nisewonger, with C Company, 2nd Battalion, 325th Airborne Infantry Regiment, 2nd Brigade Combat Team, scans a rooftop while on patrol in Adhamiyah, Baghdad. *Sgt. Michael Pryor*

military operations on urban terrain (MOUT) without compromising shooting capabilities.

The lineage of the M4A1 goes back almost five decades to the mid-1950s when the U.S. military sought a weapon to replace the heavy M14 battle rifle; in 1959 that weapon, the M16 rifle, was born. A product of Eugene Stoner, this lightweight assault weapon was viewed with apprehension when first introduced. Soldiers used to the heavy M1 and M14 rifles often referred to it as the "toy gun." As the war continued, other modifications of the M16 series were developed, and the XM177E1 was introduced to the U.S.

Sgt. Abdou Cham, a team leader with C Company, 2nd Battalion, 325th Airborne Infantry Regiment, 2nd Brigade Combat Team, pulls security while on patrol in Adhamiyah, Baghdad. He is armed with an M4A1 equipped with an Aimpoint Comp-M sight and older model AN/PEQ-4 laser-aiming device. He is also carrying a shotgun for encounters of an up-close nature, or for breaching a door. *Sgt. Michael Pryor*

troops. This was a shorter version of the M16 with a collapsible stock and various barrel lengths; it was often referred to as the CAR-15 (Colt automatic rifle-15). It saw service with the U.S. Navy SEALs, long-range recon patrols (LRRPs), a studies and observation group (SOG) in Vietnam, and other special operations solders. This carbine version of the M16 laid the groundwork for the Colt M4/M4A1 carbine in use today which has evolved into the weapon of choice for today's, special operations forces in general as well as the Airborne Infantry.

The M4A1 has a rifling twist of 1 in 7 inches, making it compatible with the full range of 5.56mm ammunitions. Its sighting system contains dual apertures, allowing for viewing from 0 to 200 meters and a smaller opening for engaging targets at a longer range, 500 to 600 meters. Selective fire controls for the M4A1 have eliminated the three-round burst, replacing it with safe, semi-automatic, and full automatic fire.

Another piece of Special Operations Command (SOCOM) equipment that is being used by the paratroopers is the special operations peculiar modification (SOPMOD) accessory kit, which allows the paratrooper to modify the weapon per mission parameters. Using the rail interface system (RIS), numerous components of the kit may be secured to the weapon. The kit includes a 4x32mm Trijicon day optical scope, allowing the soldiers to judge range and deliver more accurate fire out to 300 meters; a Trijicon reflex sight, which is designed for close-in engagement; and an infrared target pointer/illuminator/aiming laser, the AN/PEQ-2, for use with night-vision devices. It places a red aiming dot on the target, which is useful in MOUT missions. One officer commented, "When wearing night-vision goggles and using the laser, it is like the hand of God reaches out, and takes out the enemy." Additionally, it is equipped with a visible light (a high-intensity flashlight mounted on the rail system) and a backup iron sight (the carrying handle of the M4A1 can be removed, and this backup sight can be employed in the absence of the handle). The kit also contains a forward handgrip, which helps to stabilize the weapon and keeps the user's hands away from the hand guards and barrel, which tends to heat up in combat. As one of the paratroopers commented, "With all the extra stuff on the rifle, there's no room to hold the hand guard anyway." The kit also includes a sound

The paratroopers often augment their weapons with commercial, off-the-shelf (COTS) gear. In this case, the soldier has mounted a Leupold Mark 4 1-3x14mm close-quarter/tactical riflescope, and Spc. Michael Allgeier, rifleman, 3rd Platoon, Company A, 2nd Battalion, 508th Parachute Infantry Regiment, pulls security while on patrol near the town of Miri, in Ghazni province, Afghanistan. *Pfc. Micah Clare*

Sgt. Nicholas Heurich, a dismount team leader in 3rd Platoon, Troop B, 4th Squadron, 73rd Cavalry Regiment, 4th Brigade Combat Team, scouts the road ahead during a patrol near a small village in Paktika province, Afghanistan. He has modified his M4 with an after-market Vltor stock. *Pfc. Micah Clare*

suppressor, which significantly reduces the noise and flash of the muzzle blast.

Special Operations Peculiar Modification (SOPMOD) M4A1 Accessory Kit

The M4A1 carbine is a most capable and deadly weapon suitable for any paratrooper. SOCOM wanted to make the weapon even more effective, whether for close-in engagements or long-range targets. To accomplish this, SOCOM and Crane Division, Naval Surface Warfare Center, developed the SOPMOD accessory kit. Also introduced in 1994, the kit is issued to all U.S. Special Operations Forces to expand on the capabilities and operation of the M4A1 carbine. Officially it is called the SOPMOD kit, and some of the troopers continue to refer to it as such; other troopers call it simply the accessory kit.

The SOPMOD accessory kit contains numerous components that can be attached directly onto the M4A1 carbine or onto the rail interface system. The various accessories give the paratrooper the flexibility to choose the appropriate optics, lasers, lights, et cetera, depending on mission parameters. The SOPMOD kit is constantly being evaluated, and research is ongoing to further enhance the operability, functionality, and lethality of the M4A1 carbine. The paratroopers also

utilize other military and commercial off-the-shelf (COTS) modifications to enhance the M4A1 and the SOPMOD kit depending on mission parameters.

Rail Interface System (RIS)

The rail interface system (RIS), as well as the alternate rail attachment aystem (RAS), is a notched rail system that replaces the front hand guards on the M4A1 receiver. This rail system is located on the top, bottom, and sides of the barrel, which facilitates the attaching of SOPMOD kit components on any of the four sides. The notches are numbered, making it possible to attach and re-attach a component at the same position each time it is mounted. Optical sights and night-vision devices can be mounted on the top, whereas the top and side rails are the choice for positioning laser aiming devices or lights. The bottom of the RIS can usually accommodate the vertical grip and/or lights. When no accessories are mounted to the RIS, plastic hand guards are in place to cover and protect the unused portions of the rail.

Advanced Combat Optical Gunsight (ACOG)

The ACOG (advanced combat optical gunsight), manufactured by Trijicon, is the day optical scope for the SOPMOD

Staff Sgt. Jeremy Hendrix, with Bravo Company, 2nd Battalion, 505th Parachute Infantry Regiment, provides security during a search for weapons caches near the city of Ad Dwar, Iraq. His M4 is equipped with an ACOG and an AN/PEQ-2. The Trijicon ACOG (advanced combat optical gunsight) 4x32 scope, mounted on an M4A1. The ACOG is a four-power telescopic sight, including a ballistic compensating reticle. Utilizing this reticle provides increase capability to direct, identify, and hit the target to the maximum effective range of the M4A1 carbine (600 meters). *Tech. Sgt. Molly Dzitko*

The Trijicon ACOG provides increased hit potential in all lighting conditions. The exterior of the ACOG is a forged aluminum body (aircraft-strength 7075 alloy). The ACOG has internally adjustable, compact telescopic sights that use tritium-illuminated reticles for target acquisition in all light conditions. Sgt. Mark Brown, B Company, 1st Battalion, 508th Parachute Infantry Regiment, 4th Brigade Combat Team, adjusts his equipment before heading out on patrol during Operation Achilles in southern Afghanistan. *82nd Airborne Division Public Affairs Office*

A paratrooper attached to the 3rd Stryker Brigade Combat Team, 2nd Infantry Division, provides security during Operation Arrowhead Ripper, in Baqubah, Iraq. The operation is a joint effort between U.S. and Iraqi security forces to defeat al Qaeda terrorists and secure the city. The soldier pictured is from the 2nd Battalion, 505th Parachute Infantry Regiment, from Fort Bragg, North Carolina. *Sgt. Armando Monroig*

kit. The ACOG is a four-power telescopic sight that includes a ballistic compensating reticle. Utilizing this reticle provides increased capability to direct, identify, and hit targets to the maximum effective range of the M4A1 carbine (600 meters). As a backup, the ACOG is equipped with an iron sight for rapid close-range engagement (CRE). Both the front iron sight and the scope reticle provide target recognition and standoff attack advantage while retaining a close-quarters capability equivalent to that of the standard iron sights.

Visible Light Illuminator (VLI)

The visible light illuminator (VLI) provides white light to facilitate moving inside darkened buildings, bunkers, tunnels, et cetera. The white light is useful for searching for and identifying the target. The illuminator has a dual-battery capability; it can be powered by three 3-volt lithium DL 123 batteries or six 1.5-volt AA batteries. The visible light illuminator is most useful in military operations other than war, or in low-intensity conflicts, when search and clear operations may be complicated by tripwires, booby traps, or noncombatants, and the danger of revealing your position is offset by the need for better vision than is possible with night-vision goggles. The intense white light can overwhelm an opponent in MOUT, giving the soldier a momentary advantage. An infrared (IR) filter can be attached to provide short-range illumination (50 meters) when using night-vision equipment. This red filter also reduces glare in smoky environments and reduces impact on the soldier's night vision.

AN/PEQ-2 Infrared Illuminator/Aiming Laser

The AN/PEQ-2 infrared target pointer/illuminator/aiming laser (ITPIAL) allows the M4A1 to be effectively employed to 300 meters with standard-issue night-vision goggles (NVG) or a weapon-mounted night-vision device—that is, an AN/PVS-14. The IR illuminator broadens the capabilities of the NVGs in buildings, tunnels, jungle, and overcast and other low-light conditions where starlight would not be sufficient to support night vision. The illuminator also allows visibility in areas normally in shadow. At close range, a neutral density filter is used to eliminate flare around the aiming laser to improve the view of the target; the filter aids in iden-

tification as well as precision aiming. This combination provides the paratrooper a decisive advantage over an opposing force with little or no night-vision capability.

Visible Laser AN/PEQ-5

The AN/PEQ-5, as the name implies, is a visible laser (VL) that attaches to the RIS and provides a close-range visible laser aiming beam. The VL can be used at close range in a lighted building, in darkness with the visible light illuminator, or at night with night-vision equipment. It is used primarily in MOUT, where it provides a fast and accurate means of aiming the weapon. It is especially valuable when the soldier is wearing a protective mask, firing from an awkward position, or firing from behind cover and around corners. It permits the shooter to focus all his attention on the target while being able to accurately direct the point of impact. Because it is visible, it does provide a nonlethal show of force that can intimidate hostile personnel, letting the "bad guys" know that you have them in your sights.

Forward Handgrip

The forward, or vertical, handgrip attaches to the bottom of the RIS and provides added support, giving the soldier a more stable firing platform. Used as a monopod in a supported position, it allows the soldier to hold the weapon despite overheating. The forward handgrip can be used to push against the assault sling and stabilize the weapon with isometric tension during MOUT. Using the handgrip brings the shooter's elbows in closer or tighter to his body, keeping the weapon in front of him. The handgrip provides quicker handling when additional components have been attached to the weapon, thus providing more precise target acquisition.

Having numerous modifications available tends to make the soldier want to use them all. It is not uncommon to see a soldier with as wide a variety of SOPMOD accessories on the M4A1 as it can hold. One of the drawbacks of the vertical grip is the possibility of an accessory catching on a ledge of a building or the edge of the helicopter during insertion or extraction. This issue is being addressed by the evaluation of a quick-release lever on the forward grip, as well as a shorter handgrip.

The AN/PVS-14 can be used hand held, helmet mounted, or attached to the rail interface system/rail attachment system (RIS/RAS) of a weapon. Manufactured by ITT, the AN/PVS-14 offers the latest, state-of-the-art capability in a package that meets the rigorous demands of the U.S. military. By using the monocular configuration, the paratrooper can operate with a night-vision device on one eye while maintaining natural night vision in the other eye. This is a night-vision view of Pvt. Mathew Packuc, with the 82nd Airborne Division, Alpha Company, at the outer perimeter of Bagram Air Base, Afghanistan. *Staff Sgt. Cherie A. Thurlby, U.S. Air Force*

M203 Grenade Launcher

The quick attach/detach M203 mount and leaf sight, when combined with the standard M203 grenade launcher, provides additional firepower to the paratrooper, giving him a point and an area engagement capability. The most commonly utilized ammunition is the M406 40mm projectile, which includes high-explosive dual-purpose (HEDP) ammunition. This grenade, which has a deadly radius of five meters, is used as antipersonnel and anti-light armor. Additional projectiles include the M381 HE, M386 HE, M397 airburst, M397A1 airburst, M433 high-explosive dual-purpose (HEDP), M441 HE, M576 buckshot, M583A1 40mm WS PARA ILLUM, M585 white star cluster, M651 CS, M661 green star cluster, M662 red star cluster, M676 yellow smoke canopy, M680 white smoke canopy, M682 red smoke canopy, M713 ground marker red, M715 ground marker green, M716 ground marker yellow, M781 practice, M918 target practice, M992 infrared illuminant cartridge (IRIC), 40mm nonlethal round, 40mm canister round, and 40mm sponge grenade.

The sponge grenade has a deadly radius of five meters. The M433 multipurpose grenade, in addition to the fragmentation effects, is capable of penetrating steel armor plate up to two inches thick. Future developments in 40mm grenades will introduce airburst capability to provide increased lethality and bursting radius through prefragmented, programmable HE warheads.

The quick-attach M203 combines flexibility and lethality to the individual weapon. Utilizing multiple M203 setups allows concentrated fire by bursting munitions, which are extremely useful in raids and ambushes, and can illuminate or obscure the target while simultaneously delivering continuous HEDP fire. The M203 grenade leaf sight attaches to the rail interface system for fire control.

The receiver of the M203 is manufactured of high-strength forged aluminum alloy, which provides extreme ruggedness while keeping weight to a minimum. A complete self-cocking firing mechanism, including striker, trigger, and positive safety lever, is included in the receiver. This allows the M203 to be operated as an independent weapon even while it is attached to the M16A1 or M16A2 rifle

The primary rifle in use with the 82nd Airborne Division is the Colt M4A1 carbine. This shortened version of the M16A2 rifle features a collapsible stock, a flat-topped upper receiver with an accessory rail, and a detachable handle/rear aperture sight assembly. The M4A1 has a fire selector for semi- and fully automatic operation. Pfc. George Gonzalez, rifleman, 3rd Platoon, Company A, 2nd Battalion, 508th Parachute Infantry Regiment, takes a knee while on patrol near the town of Miri, in Ghazni province, Afghanistan. *Pfc. Micah Clare*

or the M4A1 carbine. The barrel is also made of high-strength aluminum alloy, which has been shortened from twelve inches to nine inches, allowing improved balance and handling. The barrel slides forward in the receiver to accept a round of ammunition, then slides backward to automatically lock in the closed position, ready to fire. The M203 brings added firepower to the already proven and outstanding M4A1 carbine.

AN/PVS14 Night-Vision Device

The AN/PVS-14D is the optimum night-vision monocular ensemble for special applications. The monocular, or pocket scope, can be hand-held, mounted on a facemask or helmet, or attached to a weapon. The new PVS-14D night-vision monocular offers the latest, state-of-the-art capability in a package that meets the rigorous demands of the paratroopers.

The EOTech holographic display sight uses the same technology that's found in the heads-up display (HUD) on the F-117 aircraft. As the name implies, the EOTech displays holographic patterns, which have been designed for instant target acquisition under any lighting situations, without covering or obscuring the point of aim. The holographic reticle can be seen through the sight, providing the soldier with a large view of the target or the zone of engagement. With both eyes open, the soldier sights in on the target for a true two-eye operation. Spc. Brad Meetze, a team leader in Company A, 2nd Battalion, 508th Parachute Infantry Regiment, provides perimeter security during a town meeting (shura) in Dey Yak, Afghanistan. *Pfc. Micah Clare*

The monocular configuration is important to shooters who want to operate with night vision while maintaining dark adaptation in the other eye. The head-mount assembly, a standard in the kit, facilitates hands-free operation when helmet wear is not required. The weapon mount allows for use in a variety of applications, from using iron sights to coupling with a red dot or tritium sighting system such as the Aimpoint Comp-M/ML, Trijicon ACOG system, and EOTech holographic display sight (HDS). A compass is available to allow the user to view the bearing in the night-vision image.

Aimpoint Comp-M

The Aimpoint Comp-M is used for MOUT activities. After extensive testing, the U.S. Army adopted the Aimpoint Comp-M as its red dot sighting system. Using a both-eyes-open and heads-up method, the shooter is able to acquire the target with excellent speed and accuracy. The Comp-M sight superimposes a red dot on the target, allowing the soldier to adjust his weapon accordingly in the fast-paced shooting environment of close-quarters battle (CQB). The Comp-M is parallax free, which means that the shooter does not have to compensate for parallax deviation. The

The heads-up, rectangular, full view of the holographic display sight (HDS) is passive and gives off no signature, which could be seen by opposing units using night-vision goggles (NVGs). The reticle, which has ten night-vision settings, will not "bloom" when viewed through night-vision equipment. When used in conjunction with the AN/PVS-14 night-vision device, the HDS provides the paratrooper with an outstanding view of the target area, and immediate target acquisition even in the darkest of environments. *Pfc. Micah Clare*

The M14 rifle was the standard U.S. service rifle until it was replaced in the late 1960s by the M16A1 rifle. Although the M14 was replaced as the standard battle rifle during the Vietnam War, it has found a new resurgence among U.S. forces. It is not uncommon to see a paratrooper carrying the M14 due to the takedown capabilities of the 7.62mm ammunition. Spc. Jason Peacock, from the 14th Cavalry Regiment, scans the rooftops from his overwatch position during a cordon-and-search mission in Baghdad. *Staff Sgt. Sean A. Foley*

sight can be mounted on the carrying handle or the RIS of the M4A1.

Holographic Display Sight (HDS)

Manufactured by EOTech, the holographic display sight (HDS), as the name implies, displays holographic patterns, which have been designed for instant target acquisition under any lighting situations without covering or obscuring the point of aim. The holographic reticle can be seen through the sight, providing the shooter with a large view of the target or zone of engagement. Unlike other optics, the HDS is passive and gives off no telltale signature. The heads-up, rectangular, full view of the HDS eliminates any blind spots,

constricted vision, or tunnel vision normally associated with cylindrical sights. With both eyes open, the shooter sights in on the target for a true two-eye operation.

The wide field of view of the HDS allows the paratrooper to sight in on the target/target area while maintaining peripheral viewing through the sight if needed, up to 350 degrees off axis. A unique feature of the HDS is that it works even if the heads-up display window is obstructed by mud, snow, et cetera. Even if the laminated window is shattered, the sight remains fully operational, with the point of aim/impact being maintained. Because many GWOT missions favor the night, the HDS can be used in conjunction with NVG/NVD. The hallmarks of the HDS are

A soldier assigned to A Company, 2nd Battalion, 504th Parachute Infantry Regiment, sights through the scope attached to his 7.62mm M21 sniper rifle during a search-and-destroy mission in the mountains of Adi Ghar, Afghanistan, during Operation Mongoose. *Sgt. 1st Class Milton H. Robinson*

speed and ease of use, equating incredible accuracy and instant sight-on-target operation, which can be the difference between life and death in MOUT operations.

M14

The M14 dates back to 1957 when the U.S. Army selected it as the standard service rifle for the infantry. It was to be a replacement for the M1 Garand and the M1918 Browning automatic rifle (BAR). Gen. George S. Patton said, "The M1 rifle is the greatest battle implement ever devised." It could be argued that the general might have a similar view of the M14 had he been around to witness its evolution.

The M14 was the main battle rifle until the late 1960s, when it was replaced by the M16 assault rifle during the Vietnam War. Although the majority of the soldiers and marines in country were issued the new "black rifle," the M14 continued to be used on a limited basis by small numbers of elite teams throughout the war.

After the war in Southeast Asia, the M14 rifles were relegated to the background, although they often appeared at competition shooting. The M16 and the newer CAR-15 versions had all but replaced the heavy wooden stocked weapon. However, the M14 found a home with the Special Operations Forces. It was not uncommon to see the heavy-

Snipers from the 508th Parachute Infantry Regiment provide security during a town meeting in Dey Yak, Afghanistan. The sniper in the foreground is equipped with a modified M14 in a Sage Industries, Ltd., stock. The updated stock provides the sniper with a Picatinny rail system for the mounting of optics, laser-aiming devices, and other accessories. The two paratroopers are part of the International Security Assistance Force (ISAF). The sniper in the background is armed with an M24 sniper weapon system with an AN/PVS-10 day- and night-vision sniper scope. *Pfc. Micah Clare*

hitting weapon among SEAL teams and Ranger platoons. Additionally, it would be used by Delta operator Sgt. 1st Class Randall Shugarht during the fateful mission of Task Force Ranger in Somalia.

The M14 rifle is a gas-operated shoulder-fired weapon that uses a 7.62mm round from a twenty-round magazine. The rifle is capable of semi-automatic and full automatic fire via a selector on the right side of the weapon. The rifle, which weighs eleven pounds with full magazine and sling, has a cyclic rate of fire of 750 rounds per minute with an effective range of 400 meters. Variations of the standard M14 can be seen in the designated marksman rifle as well as the M21 and the enhanced battle rifle.

M21

The M21 is a product of the Vietnam War, developed jointly by the Army Weapons Command, Rock Island, Illinois; the Combat Development Command, Fort Benning, Georgia; and the Limited Warfare Agency, Aberdeen, Maryland. During the Vietnam War, the M21 was the primary sniper rifle of the U.S. Army and remained so until replaced by the M24 sniper weapon system (SWS) in 1988. The M21 remains in service with the 82nd Airborne Division as well as other elite and some SOF units. The M21 7.62mm SWS consists of a national match M14 barrel and scope. The M21 is accurized by the U.S. Army Marksmanship Training Unit and shares the basic specifications and operations of the

The M24 sniper weapon system (SWS) was fielded in 1988. Based on a Remington 700 action for 7.62mm ammunition, the receiver was made adjustable to take the .300 Winchester magnum round. The M24 is equipped with a Leupold Mark 4 ten-power fixed M3A scope, referred to as the "Ma-3 Alpha." A detachable bipod, in this case a Harris, can be attached to the stock's fore end. The M24 SWS is a bolt-action rifle capable of engaging a target well over 500 meters away. Spc. Jesse Nangauta, a sniper with Headquarters and Headquarters Troop (HHT), 1/73 Cav, takes aim at an enemy target from his concealed position during a field training exercise (FTX). *Sgt. Michael Pryor*

standard M14. The significant differences in the M21 include a barrel (which is not chromium plated) that is selected and gauged to ensure specific tolerances. The stock of the weapon is impregnated with epoxy and the receiver is individually fitted to the walnut stock with a fiberglass compound. The gas cylinder and piston are modified and polished to reduce carbon buildup and improve the operation of the weapon.

Enhanced Battle Rifle

This modified M14 was a result of the small-arms section of the U.S. Navy Crane Surface Warfare Center to give a new lease on life to the M14 assault rifle. Crane teamed up with Sage Industries, Ltd., to create the enhanced battle rifle (EBR). Originally designed by Crane for the SEAL and Marine Force Recon community, the EBR has found

A sniper from the 82nd Airborne Division trains on the new XM110 semi-automatic sniper system (SASS) held at Forward Operating Base Salerno, Afghanistan. The SASS will be added to the arsenal of weapons that the soldiers of Task Force Fury have at their disposal, including the older style M24 SWS, seen here in the foreground. The SASS, which will replace the aging M24 SWS, fires a 7.52mm round from a five-, ten-, or twenty-round magazine. *Spc. Matthew Leary*

its way into many of the conventional units. The EBR uses a unique Sage stock that allows the barrel, receiver, and trigger group to be installed. The stock features four Mil-Standard 1913 Picatinny rails that surround the barrel and an additional rail above the receiver to accommodate the placement of night-vision devices and other optics. The Sage stock incorporates a pistol grip and a retractable stock, which facilitates the length of pull (LOP), and check weld for the shooter.

The EBR, without scope or added devices, weighs less than twelve pounds, with a 22-inch regular M14 barrel. The addition of the Sage stock provides the shooter with a straight line over the previous wooden stock, reducing the felt recoil of the 7.62mm round.

M24 Sniper Weapon System (SWS)

The current-issue sniper rifle for the army is the M24 sniper weapon system. The M24 is based on the Remington 700 series long action. This action accommodates chambering for either the 7.62x51mm or the .300 Winchester magnum round. The rifle is a bolt-action six-shot repeating rifle (one

round in the chamber and five additional rounds in the magazine). It is issued with the Leupold Mark 4 ten-power M3A scope, commonly referred to as the "Ma-3-Alpha." In addition, the sniper can make use of the metallic iron sights. Attached to the scope is the M24/EMA anti-reflection device (ARD). Less than three inches long, this honeycomb of tubes cuts down the glare of the scope. The M24 SWS comes with a Harris bipod; however, most of the time the bipod remains in the deployment case. The rifle weighs 12.1 pounds without the scope; it has an overall length of 43 inches, with a 24-inch free-floating barrel. The stock is a composite of Kevlar, graphite, and fiberglass with an aluminum-bedding block. The stock has an adjustable butt plate to accommodate the length of pull.

82nd Airborne Snipers in Iraq

In a report from the 82nd Airborne Division Public Affairs Office, Spc. Ryan Cannon, a sniper deployed in Operation Iraqi Freedom, related that he didn't think there is anything particularly unusual about what he does for a living. It's just a job, Cannon says. But most people's jobs don't require them to shoot people with a high-powered rifle from hundreds of meters away. Specialist Cannon is a sniper with Scout Platoon, Headquarters Company, 3rd Battalion, 325th Airborne Infantry Regiment, 82nd Airborne Division.

Since arriving in Iraq in December, the scouts have made a crucial contribution to the battalion's mission by conducting surveillance and reconnaissance of anti-Iraqi forces and providing precision long-range cover fire during every major combat operation. The scouts are an invaluable combat multiplier on the battlefield in a variety of ways. The 82nd could not be successful without the efforts of the scout teams; battalion commander Lt. Col. Thomas Hiebert thinks they're the best in the business.

Hiebert's affection for the scouts is no mystery; they're known as the eyes and ears of the commander. Scout missions range from pure reconnaissance to straight sniper operations. One assignment might require them to stay on a rooftop for days, tracking the comings and goings of suspected insurgents with zoom lenses, video cameras, and thermal imaging devices. Another assignment might involve only a few hours of work providing cover for a patrol.

The M249 squad automatic weapon (SAW) is an individually portable, air-cooled, belt-fed, gas-operated light machine gun that fires from the open-bolt position. Pfc. Jordan Rud, with the 82nd Airborne Division's long-range surveillance detachment (LRSD), fires a 5.56mm M249 SAW downrange during Operation Enduring Freedom. The weapon is equipped with a fixed stock and an Elcan sight. *Cpl. Jeremy Colvin*

The scouts really earn their paychecks when the battalion conducts raids or cordon-and-search operations in unsecured areas of Baghdad. On those occasions, the scouts move covertly into the area in advance of the main effort, hunker down inside a building with a good view of the sector, and, with their .50-caliber and 7.62mm sniper weapons systems, provide protection for troopers moving on the ground.

When the snipers acquire a target, they must receive authorization from the tactical commander before they can shoot. After that, the ball is in their hands and they don't hesitate. Says scout platoon leader Lt. Jaime Clark, "Every AIF [anti-Iraqi forces] we can positively identify and kill is one less guy who can throw a hand grenade or take a shot at our forces. We make the area a lot safer for our troops, Iraqi security forces, and for innocent Iraqi civilians."

All the scouts have stories about shots they've taken. Specialist Cannon once zeroed in on the cherry of a cigarette being smoked by an insurgent who was about to fire a mortar from five hundred meters away; Cannon took him out—at night. "That's a pretty difficult shot," he said—a decided understatement. Spc. Scott Kuzminski once shot a moving insurgent who was firing an AK-47 from behind a building more than two hundred meters away, despite having an area of visibility to aim at that was only the size of a comic book.

Because targets usually have no idea that they're in a scout's sights, the snipers have time to consider the consequences of what they're doing before they fire. It's not something that troubles them. "I don't have a problem pulling the trigger," said Cannon. "There's no ethical reasoning that goes through my head. That guy is just a threat that needs to be eliminated." The scouts leave the moral calculations to the commanders. Said Cannon,

once scouts get the green light to engage a target, they have no problem fulfilling their duties. Kuzminski said that when scouts are out on a mission, their responsibility is to make sure the people patrolling the area are safe. Everyone takes it seriously because chances are it's their friend down there.

The standard ammunition load for the M249 is two hundred rounds of 5.56mm ammunition in disintegrating belts that alternate four rounds of full metal jacket and one round of tracer. These rounds are fed from a two-hundred-round plastic ammunition box and through the side of the weapon. The M249 has a regulator for selecting a normal (750 rounds per minute) or maximum (1,000 rounds per minute) rate of fire. Pfc. Ryan Cole, a paratrooper with D Company, 2nd Battalion, 325th Airborne Infantry Regiment, 2nd Brigade Combat Team, pulls security during the dedication ceremony for a renovated school in Al Beida, in the Adhamiyah district of Baghdad. The M249 has a collapsible stock and an Aimpoint sight. *Sgt. Michael Pryor*

M110 Semi-Automatic Sniper System

The paratroopers have begun to field a new sniper rifle, the M110 semi-automatic sniper system (SASS). The rifle itself is manufactured by Knight's Armament Company (KAC) in Titusville, Florida. The complete system includes Leupold daytime optics, a Harris swivel bipod, an AN/PVS14 night sight, and other SOPMOD accessories. The rifle has ambidextrous features, such as a double-sided magazine release and safety selector switch.

Based on the design of the original AR10 by Eugene Stoner, the M110 is much more than an M16 on steroids. The rifle is similar to Knight's SR-25 and the Mk 11 Mod 0 semi-automatic precision rifle but differs significantly in buttstock and rail system design. The M110 features

A gunner's view of Afghanistan. The squad automatic weapon (SAW) can utilize standard twenty- and thirty-round M4/M16 magazines, which are inserted into a magazine well in the bottom of the SAW. Utilizing the same 5.56mm ammunition as the M4, the SAW allows the teams to carry common ammunition loads. The M249 is capable of engaging targets out to 800 meters. A paratrooper assigned to A Company, 2nd Battalion, 504th Parachute Infantry Regiment, armed with a 5.56mm M249 SAW, provides security during a search-and-destroy mission in the mountains of Adi Ghar, Afghanistan, during Operation Mongoose. *Sgt. 1st Class Milton H. Robinson*

Pvt. Michael Ryan (right) and Pfc. Branigan Kerr provide security on the roof of a home in the Adhamiyah district of Baghdad. The infantrymen, with Company B, 2nd Battalion, 325th Parachute Infantry Regiment, patrolled the neighborhoods around Combat Outpost Callahan as part of the new Baghdad Security Plan. Private Ryan is armed with the M240B, which is the replacement for the older M60 machine gun. The M240 is equipped with an ACOG sight and an AN/PEQ-2. *Sgt. Michael Garrett*

additional refinements designed by KAC to maximize parts commonality with the AR15/M16, improve weapon reliability, and increase accuracy.

The M110 SASS is a rapid fire/rapid reload sniper rifle with an enhanced sniper spotting scope system; folding detachable bipod; five-, ten-, and twenty-round-capacity detachable magazines; barrel life greater than five thousand rounds; variable-power day optical scope; detachable weapon suppressor; integrated Mil-Standard 1913 rail system; and hard case for storage and transportation. In addition, the M110 weighs less than the M24 SWS, its rate of fire and lethality exceed that of the M24, and it's primarily antipersonnel at ranges equal to or greater than the M24.

Paratroopers from Task Force Fury, located at Forward Operating Base (FOB) Salerno, Afghanistan, have fielded a new sniper rifle, the XM110 semi-automatic sniper system. The paratroopers of the 82nd Airborne Division are among the first soldiers to receive the new weapon system in a combat zone.

The new rifle has several new features, but the most prominent is its improved rate of fire. According to Staff Sgt. Jason Terry, a sniper instructor at the U.S. Army Sniper School, "It's semi-automatic, so it allows for rapid

re-engagement of targets. Older style rifles, such as the commonly used M24 sniper weapon system, are bolt-action weapons that require the sniper to manually feed another round into the chamber after each shot. The automatic firing capabilities of the SASS will cut down on the lag time in between shots. Snipers have a unique role within the army, going out in pairs and conducting reconnaissance and providing long-range precision fire in support of missions."

Commented Pfc. Joel D. Dulashanti, a sniper with Troop C, 4th Squadron, 73rd Cavalry Regiment, 4th Brigade Combat Team, 82nd Airborne Division, "Because of their movement in small groups, snipers focus on being undetected by the enemy."

Because of this need for stealth, the M110 SASS has also been configured to accept a suppressor. This not only lowers the noise level of the weapon, it significantly reduces the muzzle blast, which could give away the position of the sniper team. The enhancement makes locating snipers in the field, even after they have fired a shot, difficult for enemy forces.

Staff Sgt. Terry and a team of other specialists traveled along with the equipment as the weapon was deployed among the units, and provided training on the SASS. Terry

Spc. Eric McManus (left) and Spc. Nathan Ihrcke, paratroopers with D Company, 2nd Battalion, 325th Airborne Infantry Regiment, 2nd Brigade Combat Team, pull security during the dedication ceremony for a new soccer field in Al Beida, in the Adhamiyah district of Baghdad. Specialist McManus is armed with the M240B machine gun, a highly reliable 7.62mm weapon that delivers more energy to the target than the smaller-caliber M249 squad automatic weapon The M240B has an effective range of more than one mile with a cyclic rate of fire of 650 to 950 rounds per minute. *Sgt. Michael Pryor*

and his team ran the soldiers through a three-day training course to familiarize them with the operation and maintenance of the new weapon. Terry stated, "Most of those in the class had already been to the U.S. Army Sniper School, so the introduction of the new weapon merely augmented the snipers' arsenal. We brought [the M110s] into the country with us, and they'll stay here. Getting the soldiers comfortable with the SASS was the exact purpose of the training."

Said Spc. Aaron J. Fillmore, "The training provides a better understanding of the weapon and reassured the soldiers of its use." Fillmore, an infantryman with Troop C,

4/73 Cavalry, has been assigned to the sniper section. "I think it's a pretty simple gun to maintain and operate," he said. "It was good to get the familiarization with the weapon."

Said Staff Sgt. Jose L. Galvan, a sniper instructor from the U.S. Army Sniper School, "In the end, it's about providing competent and accurate fire and reconnaissance for maneuver units while they conduct operations here." The semi-automatic fire provided by the XM110 SASS is a notable improvement. "They now have a semi-automatic weapon that can shoot out to the ranges of a sniper rifle," said Galvan.

The M136 AT4 is a lightweight, self-contained, man-portable, antiarmor weapon. Inside the expendable one-piece fiberglass-wrapped tube is a free-flight, fin-stabilized, rocket-type cartridge. The launcher is watertight for ease of transportation and storage. Unlike the M72 series LAAW, the AT4 launcher does not need to be extended before firing. With a range of 2,100 meters, the warhead is capable of penetrating 400 millimeters of rolled homogenous armor. *U.S. Army*

M249 Squad Automatic Weapon (SAW)

Fielded in the mid-1980s, the M249 squad automatic weapon (SAW) is an individually portable, air-cooled, belt-fed, gas-operated light machine gun. A unique feature of the SAW is the number of alternate ammunition feeds. The standard ammunition load is two hundred rounds of 5.56mm ammunition in disintegrating belts. These rounds are fed from a two-hundred-round plastic ammunition box and through the side of the weapon. The normal link ammunition for the SAW is four rounds of M855 ball ammunitions followed by one round of M85 tracer. Additionally, the weapon can utilize standard twenty- and thirty-round M16 magazines, which are inserted into a magazine well in the bottom of the SAW. Utilizing the same 5.56mm ammunition as the M4A1, the M249 allows the paratroopers to carry common ammunition loads. The M249 is capable of engaging targets out to 800 meters.

M240B Medium Machine Gun

After extensive operational testing, the U.S. Army selected the M240B medium machine gun as a replacement for the M60 family of machine guns. Manufactured by Fabrique Nationale, the 24.2-pound M240B medium machine gun is a gas-operated, air-cooled, linked-belt-fed weapon that fires 7.62x51mm rounds. The weapon fires from an open-bolt position with a maximum effective range of 1,100 meters. The rate of fire is adjustable from 750 to 1,400 rounds per minute through an adjustable gas regulator. The M240B features a folding bipod that attaches to the receiver, a quick-change barrel assembly, a feed cover and bolt assembly that enable closure of the cover regardless of bolt position, a plastic buttstock, and an integral optical sight rail. Although the M240B has many of the same characteristics as the older M60, the durability of the M240 system results in superior reliability and maintainability.

AT4

The M136 AT4 is the army's principal light antitank weapon, providing precision delivery of an 84mm high-explosive antiarmor warhead, with negligible recoil. The M136 AT4 is a man-portable, self-contained antiarmor weapon consisting of a free-flight, fin-stabilized, rocket-

The claymore mine spreads a fan-shape pattern of steel balls in a 60-degree horizontal arc at a maximum height of 2 meters, and covers a casualty radius of 100 meters. The optimum effective range is 50 meters. The forward danger radius for friendly forces is 250 meters. The back-blast area is unsafe in unprotected areas 16 meters to the rear and sides of the munition. Pfc. Derrick Wilkerson, D Company, 2nd Battalion, 325th Airborne Infantry Regiment, 2nd Brigade Combat Team, sets up a claymore mine during the expert infantry badge testing. *Pfc. Susan Blair*

type cartridge packed in an expendable one-piece fiberglass-wrapped tube. Unlike the M72 light anti-armor weapon (LAAW), the AT4 launcher does not need to be extended before firing. When the warhead makes impact with the target, the nose cone crushes and the impact sensor activates the internal fuse. Upon ignition, the piezoelectric fuse element triggers the detonator, initiating the main charge. This results in penetration where the main charge fires and sends the warhead body into a directional gas jet, which

is capable of penetrating more than seventeen inches of armor plate. The aftereffects are "spalling" the projecting of fragments; the incendiary effects generate blinding light and obliterate the interior of the target.

M18A1 Claymore Mine

The M18A1 mine, more commonly referred to as the claymore mine, is primarily employed as a defensive weapon; however, it has been used in certain situations as an offensive

Soldiers assigned to Alpha Company fire an M83A3 illumination round from their 60mm M224 lightweight company mortar to get a better look at the outer perimeter of Bagram Air Base, Afghanistan, during Operation Enduring Freedom. *Staff Sgt. Cherie A. Thurlby, U.S. Air Force*

Command Sgt. Maj. Klaus J. Meckenstock, the senior noncommissioned officer with 1st Battalion, 504th Parachute Infantry Regiment, hangs an 81mm mortar round during the platoon's registration at Forward Operating Base Loyalty. *Spc. Courtney Marulli*

weapon. It can also be deployed as a booby trap and can be used as a pursuit deterrence device. It has the capability of being sighted directionally to provide fragmentation over a specific target area, and it can be command detonated.

The M18A1 antipersonnel mine is a curved rectangular plastic case that contains a layer of composition C3 explosive. Packed in the explosive are seven hundred steel balls. The front face of the case, which contains the steel balls, is designed to produce an arc-shape spray, which can be aimed at a predetermined target area. The mine comes in a bandoleer, which includes the M18A1 mine, an M57 firing device, an M40 test set, and an electrical blasting cap assembly.

M224 60mm Mortar

The M224 60mm lightweight mortar is a smooth-bore, muzzle-loading, high-angle-of-fire weapon. Its purpose is to provide the company commander with an indirect-fire weapon. The cannon assembly is composed of the barrel, combination base cap, and firing mechanism. The mount consists of a bipod and a base plate, which is provided with screw-type elevating and traversing mechanisms to elevate/ traverse the mortar. The M64 sight unit is attached to the bipod mount via a standard dovetail. An additional short-range sight is attached to the base of the cannon tube for firing the mortar on the move and during assaults. The

mortar has a spring-type shock absorber to absorb the shock of recoil in firing. The complete mortar weighs 46.5 pounds and has an effective range out to 3,500 meters.

M252 81mm Mortar

The M252 81mm mortar is a medium extended-range indirect-fire weapon weighing 91 pounds. This three-man crew-served weapon is extremely accurate out to 5,700 meters. The muzzle end of the barrel has a short tape that servers as a blast attenuator; the breach end is finned for improved cooling. The M252 system consists of the M253 cannon (tube), M177 mortar mount, M3A1 base plate, and M64A1 sight unit. The mortar provides long-range indirect-fire support to light infantry, air assault, and airborne units across the entire battalion front with sufficient range to engage targets out to the limit of the battalion zone of influence. It is capable of firing a variety of NATO-standard ammunition, including high explosive, red phosphorus/smoke, and illumination.

M198 Towed Howitzer (155mm)

The M198 provides the soldiers of the 82nd Airborne Division with the destructive, suppressive, and protective indirect and direct field artillery fires in support of combined-arms operations. Commonly towed by a 5-ton truck, the M198 system can also be dropped by parachute or transported by a CH-47 Chinook helicopter or a C-130 aircraft.

The carriage of the M198 has a retractable suspension system; it also has a top carriage that can be rotated 180 degrees to decrease the overall length for shipment or storage. The fire-control equipment can be used by one or two crewmen for direct or indirect fire. The gunner, on the left-hand side, controls left and right (traversing) settings; the assistant gunner, on the right-hand side, controls up and down (elevation) settings. The M198 fires all current 155mm NATO-standard ammunition, including high explosive (HE); smoke, including hexachloroethane (HC) and white phosphorus (WP); dual-purpose improved conventional munitions (DPICM); family of scatterable mines (FASCAM); cannon-launched guided projectiles (Copperhead); and illumination. Worth noting is the fact that HE rounds weigh 95 pounds. The M198 has a crew of ten and an effective range out to 2,300 meters.

M998 High-Mobility Multipurpose Wheeled Vehicle (HMMWV)

The M998 high-mobility multipurpose wheeled vehicle (HMMWV) is a military four-wheel-drive (4WD) vehicle designed and manufactured by AM General. It was designed to replace the M151 quarter-ton military utility tactical truck (MUTT), the M561 "Gama Goat," as well as the M718A1 and M792 ambulance versions, the commercial utility cargo vehicle (CUCV), and other light trucks in service with the U.S. military. The HMMWV is also in service with various other countries and organizations. The vehicle is commonly referred to as a Humvee, or Hummer, though the latter term usually refers to the civilian model sport utility vehicle (SUV) now manufactured by General Motors.

Artillerymen from B Battery, 2nd Battalion, 319th Airborne Field Artillery Regiment, 2nd Brigade Combat Team, prepare to fire a 105mm Howitzer after it—and they—were parachuted onto the battlefield during a heavy drop exercise at Drop Zone Sicily, Fort Bragg, North Carolina. *Sgt. Michael Pryor*

In June 1981 the army awarded AM General a contract to develop several prototype vehicles to be delivered to the U.S. government for a series of tests. The company was later awarded the initial production contract for fifty-five thousand HMMWVs to be delivered in 1985. The HMMWVs first saw combat in Operation Just Cause, the U.S. invasion of Panama in 1989. The HMMWV has become the vehicular backbone of U.S. forces around the world.

The HMMWV is built in a number of variations. The M998 is the baseline vehicle for the M998 series of 1 1/4-ton trucks, which are known as the HMMWV vehicles. These vehicles include eleven variants: the M998 cargo/troop carrier; the M1038 cargo/troop carrier with

U.S. Army soldiers with Delta Company, 2nd Battalion, 505th Parachute Infantry Regiment, take a break and prepare for routine weapons training near the city of Samarra, Iraq. The HMMWV has been up-armored, providing the paratroopers with greater protection from small-arms fire and improvised explosive devices (IED).
Tech. Sgt. Molly Dzitko, U.S. Air Force

Soldiers from B Company, 1st Battalion, 325th Airborne Infantry Regiment, 2nd Brigade Combat Team, prepare their equipment and vehicles before a combined mission with Iraqi Army troops on Forward Operating Base Independence, Iraq. *Staff Sgt. Martin K. Newton*

winch; the M1043 armament carrier; the M1044 armament carrier with winch; the M1045 TOW carrier; the M1046 TOW carrier with winch; the M997 ambulance, basic armor 4-litter; the M1035 ambulance, 2-litter; the M1037 shelter carrier; the M1042 shelter carrier with winch; and the M1097 heavy HMMWV (with a payload of 4,400 pounds). All HMMWVs are designed for use over all types of roads in all weather conditions and are extremely effective in the most difficult terrain. The HMMWVs high power-to-weight ratio, four-wheel drive, and high ground clearance give it outstanding cross-country mobility.

The HMMWV is 15 feet long, 7 feet wide, and 6 feet high (the latter is reducible to 4 1/2 feet). Weighing 5,200 pounds, it can be airlifted by helicopter. The power plant is a V8 6.2-liter displacement, fuel-injected diesel; it is liquid cooled and has a compression ignition. The HMMWV can ford just less than

three feet of water without any preparation; with the addition of a deepwater fording kit, it can ford five feet of water. With a fuel capacity of 25 gallons, it has a range of 350 highway miles with a cruising speed of up to 65 miles per hour.

As the U.S. military conducted missions in support of Operation Enduring Freedom and Iraqi Freedom, the soldiers encountered attacks on their vehicles by improvised explosive devices (IED). These IEDs could be as simple as an antivehicle mine or more elaborate and powerful explosives detonated by insurgents via various triggers such as cell phones. The use of the demolitions is varied because the insurgents place the devices in an assortment of ways. Some IEDs have been placed in old abandoned cars along the army's convoy route; other larger devices have been buried under roadways. The IEDs were commonly positioned to attack the soft sides or the flat bottom of the HMMWV.

A soldier of the 82nd Airborne's reconnaissance and surveillance team pulls security for the team along Alternate Supply Route Orlando near Ad Diwaniyah, Iraq. This up-armored HMMWV is fitted with an M2 .50-caliber machine gun. *Sgt. Rob Summitt*

Either method was extremely lethal during these operations, and took its toll on U.S. and coalition forces.

It was clear to the soldiers on the ground and eventually the war planners that the HMMWV was not designed for these types of attacks. They were not built for armored reconnaissance; they were built for moving troops, for convoy escort, and for armed conflict in an urban environment. Mogadishu proved that point. In light of this threat, the soldiers did what good soldiers have done for centuries; they adapted and improvised. It became a common sight

to see a HMMWV with boilerplate welded to the sides of the cargo compartment or doors. Piles of sandbags filled the cargo areas and interior of the already cramped vehicles.

Eventually the M998 would receive a substantial modification and evolve into the M1114 up-armored HMMWV. Instead of building a new vehicle, the HMMWV received an assortment of added armor attached strategically around it. The modified M1114 provides the paratroopers with 360 degrees of ballistic protection from IED, mine blast, and overhead burst. In addition to the new armor and anti-IED

Spc. Jonathan Boynton, an Mk 19 gunner in 3rd Platoon, Troop B, 4th Squadron, 73rd Cavalry Regiment, 4th Brigade Combat Team, pulls guard near a small village in Paktika province, Afghanistan. *Pfc. Micah Clare*

Mk 19 40mm Grenade Machine Gun

The Mk 19 40mm grenade machine gun is a self-powered, air-cooled, disintegrating belt-fed, blowback-operated fully automatic weapon. It is designed to deliver significant firepower against enemy personnel and lightly armored vehicles. It can be used in place of the M2 machine gun or to augment the heavy weapon.

The weapon fires a variety of 40mm grenades. The M430 HEDP 40mm grenade is capable of piercing up to two inches of armor, and it produces fragments to kill personnel within five meters and wound personnel within fifteen meters of the point of impact. Other system components include an Mk 64 cradle mount, an MOD 5, an M3 tripod mount, and an AN/TVS-5 night-vision sight. The complete weapon system weighs 137 pounds and has a rate of fire of 325 round per minute. The maximum range of the gun is 2,200 meters.

Global Positioning System (GPS)

The global positioning system is a collection of satellites that orbit the Earth twice a day. During this orbiting the satellites transmit the precise time, latitude, longitude, and altitude. Using a GPS receiver, soldiers can determine their exact location anywhere on Earth.

The GPS was developed by the U.S. Department of Defense in the early 1970s to provide a continuous, worldwide positioning and navigational system for U.S. military forces around the globe. The complete constellation, as it is called, consists of twenty-four satellites orbiting approximately twelve thousand miles above the Earth. These twenty-two active and two reserve, or backup, satellites provide data twenty-four hours a day for 2D and 3D positioning anywhere on the planet. Each satellite constantly broadcasts the precise time and location data. Troops using a GPS receiver can receive these signals. The greater the number of satellites and the more dynamic the positions, the easier it is to determine a person's location.

By measuring the time interval of the transmission and the receiving of the satellite signal, the GPS receiver calculates the distance between the user and each satellite. Using the distance measurements of at least three satellites in an algorithm computation, the GPS receiver can provide the

devices, the gunner's position has been modified to encapsulate the soldiers, protecting them from IEDs, small-arms fire, and even the occasional wire that the insurgents like to run across the streets as neck height.

M2 .50-Caliber Machine Gun

The Browning M2 .50-caliber machine gun has been serving American soldiers since the late 1920s. Referred to as "Ma Deuce" or simply the "fifty-cal," this heavy machine gun definitely puts the fear of God into the enemy. The M2 .50-caliber machine gun, with heavy barrel, is a crew-served, recoil-operated, air-cooled automatic machine gun. It may be fed from either side by reconfiguring some of the component parts. A disintegrating metallic link belt is used to feed the ammunition into the weapon.

This gun has a back plate with spade grips, a trigger, and a bolt latch release. It can be mounted on ground mounts and most vehicles as an antipersonnel and antiaircraft weapon. The gun is equipped with a leaf-type rear sight, a flash suppressor, and a spare barrel assembly. Associated components are the M63 antiaircraft mount and the M3 tripod. The weapon is rather large—62 inches long and weighing 84 pounds. It has an effective range of 2,000 meters with a maximum range of more than four miles.

precise location. Using a special encryption signal results in precise positioning service (PPS), which is used by the military. A second signal, called standard positioning service (SPS), is available for civilian and commercial use.

The infantryman uses the Rockwell "Plugger," or PSN-11. The precise name for the unit is PLGR+96 (precise lightweight GPS receiver). The PLGR96 is the most advanced version of the U.S. Department of Defense handheld GPS unit.

Secure (Y-code) differential GPS (SDGPS) allows the user to accept differential correction without zeroing the unit. Differential accuracy can be less than one meter. Other features of the Plugger include wide-area GPS enhancement (WAGE) for autonomous positioning accuracy to four meters circular error probable (CEP), jammer direction finding, targeting interface with laser range finder, remote display terminal capability, and advanced user interface features.

Weighing a mere 2.7 pounds (with batteries installed), the GPS unit is easily stowed in the rucksack or a modular lightweight load-carrying equipment (MOLLE) pouch. In addition to a handheld operation, the PLGR+96 unit can be installed into various vehicles and airborne platforms.

Rappelling

In the early days of World War II, soldiers used ropes to operate in mountainous terrain. This old mountaineering technique still has its place in the modern infantrymen's skill set. Whether working in the mountains or in an urban environment, rappelling is a valuable skill.

The soldiers of the 82nd Airborne Division train in this procedure with full combat gear; they also practice rappelling with a casualty. Attaching a regular military assault line through carabineers, or using a specially designed rappelling device known as a figure eight, soldiers can negotiate down the side of a mountain like mountain goats.

Fast Rope Insertion/Extraction System (FRIES)

The fast rope insertion/extraction system (FRIES) is the way to "insert" an assault force on the ground in seconds. This system begins with small woven ropes made of wool that are then braided into a larger rope. The rope is rolled into a deployment bag and the end secured to the helicopter. Depending on the model of chopper, the bag is just outside on the hoist mechanism of the side door or attached to a bracket off the back ramp. Once the chopper is over the insertion point, the rope is deployed. Even as it is hitting the ground, the soldiers in the chopper are jumping onto the woolen line and sliding down—the way a fireman goes down a pole. Once the team is safely on the ground, the flight engineer or the gunner (depending on the type of helicopter) pulls the safety pin, and the rope falls to the ground. Such a system is extremely useful in the rapid deployment of personnel; an entire platoon can be inserted within twelve to fifteen seconds. FRIES is the most accepted way of getting a force onto the ground expeditiously. Unlike rappelling, once the trooper hits the ground, he is free of the rope and can begin his mission immediately.

Chapter 5

COMBAT AVIATION BRIGADE

Crew members from the General Support Aviation Battalion, 82nd Combat Aviation Brigade, wait as their UH-60 Black Hawk helicopter is refueled at Forward Operating Base Fenty, in the Nangarhar province of Afghanistan. *Staff Sgt. Michael Bracken*

The 2nd Battalion (Assault), 82nd Aviation Regiment, traces its origins back to the 82nd Aviation Company in 1957. The company quickly expanded into battalion strength and in 1960 became the first combat aviation battalion organic to a division-size unit. Battlefield mobility, also referred to as air assault, had become a new focus in the 82nd Airborne Division and the 82nd Aviation Battalion, which were vanguards in these types of operations.

In 1965 the battalion received its trial by fire when a company was deployed to the Republic of Vietnam in support of the 173rd Airborne Brigade. While deployed in Vietnam, aviation crews of the 82nd conducted air assaults, combat resupply under enemy fire, and the first combat extraction of wounded soldiers from dense jungle using only a lowered rope and Swiss seats. The remainder of the 82nd Aviation Battalion deployed to the Dominican Republic in 1965 to fly airlift, reconnaissance, medical evacuation, and support psychological warfare operations.

Throughout the 1970s and 1980s, the battalion underwent numerous organizational changes to meet the rapidly evolving aviation requirements of the division. In 1979, the unit was designated the 82nd Combat Aviation Battalion; it consisted of 114 aircraft, including UH-1

U.S. Army captain Tyson Hise and Chief Warrant Officer Semi Lemafa, both from the General Support Aviation Battalion 3, 82nd Combat Aviation Brigade, inspect their UH-60 Black Hawk helicopter prior to takeoff at Bagram Air Base, in the Parwan province of Afghanistan. *Staff Sgt. Michael Bracken*

Sgt. David Hickman guides his UH-60 Black Hawk helicopter from the General Support Aviation Battalion 3, 82nd Combat Aviation Brigade, as it takes off from a mountaintop overlooking Bagram, in the Parwan province of Afghanistan. *Staff Sgt. Michael Bracken*

Hueys, AH-1 Cobras, and OH-58 Kiowa observation helicopters. In 1981 the battalion began to take delivery of a new aircraft, the UH-60A Black Hawk. It would be during Operation Urgent Fury, in October 1983, when the Black Hawk would be deployed for the first time in combat. The battalion deployed to the small Caribbean island of Grenada and led the way on a major combat air assault and numerous resupply and air movement operations.

In 1987, to meet the still expanding aviation requirements of the division, the 82nd Aviation Battalion was designated the 2nd Battalion, 82nd Aviation Regiment, within the newly formed 82nd Combat Aviation Brigade (CAB). The 2nd Battalion consisted of a headquarters company, three line companies, and a maintenance company; it has remained relatively unchanged and is the backbone of the 82nd Aviation Brigade. Shortly after this change, in 1988, the battalion deployed with the brigade to Honduras to provide support to Southern Command throughout Central America. The deployment was highlighted by survival, escape, resistance, evasion (SERE) training, deck landing qualification, mountain training, and M60-D aerial gunnery live-fire exercises.

A helicopter lands to extract Iraqi and coalition forces soldiers from an area north of Baghdad after they completed a search of the area for weapons caches. The troops found and destroyed what they suspected was an insurgent training area. *25th Combat Aviation Brigade Public Affairs Office*

In December 1989 the battalion took part in combat missions during Operation Just Cause, the invasion of Panama. The unit found itself in harm's way again in 1991 as it deployed to the Persian Gulf. Upon redeployment from Desert Shield and Desert Storm, the battalion maintained an extraordinary operational tempo. Throughout the 1990s it participated in multiple deployments to the National Training Center at Fort Irwin, California, and the Joint Readiness Training Center at Fort Chaffee, Arkansas. The battalion also assisted in the 1992 relief operations in Florida after Hurricane Andrew and flew in support of Operation Uphold Democracy in the Bahamas during 1994. Elements of the battalion conducted multiple tours in Bosnia-Herzegovina for Operation Joint Guard in 1997, and participated in continued peacekeeping operations later in 2001.

After the September 11, 2001, attacks on the United States, the battalion was again deployed to foreign soil in Afghanistan and Iraq in support of the global war on terrorism. The battalion, less Alpha Company and part of Delta Company, deployed in July 2002 as a composite aviation task force in support of Operation Enduring Freedom. Here in the mountains of Afghanistan, the battalion provided combat, combat support, and combat service support to the coalition partners to destroy Taliban and al Qaeda terrorist forces. Relieved by Alpha Company

A Black Hawk helicopter from the 82nd Airborne Combat Aviation Brigade transports a 105mm howitzer via a sling load. *82nd Airborne Division Public Affairs Office*

and Delta Company Headquarters/Headquarters Company, Bravo, Charlie, and Delta companies returned to Fort Bragg. Missions in Afghanistan included inserting and extracting scout and long-range surveillance teams in mountainous terrain at night using night-vision goggles; the missions were often on rock outcroppings too small to actually land a Black Hawk.

In September 2003 the 2nd Battalion deployed with the 82nd Aviation Brigade to Iraq in support of Operation Iraqi Freedom. The 2nd Battalion, with a force of fifteen UH-60 Black Hawk helicopters and roughly two hundred soldiers, was to support the 82nd Airborne Division in its mission to defeat insurgents and neutralize destabilizing influences in Iraq. The efforts of the 2nd Battalion contributed signifi-

cantly to helping create a secure environment for the people of Iraq and a safe governing backdrop for the Coalition Provisional Authority.

By June 2004 with the return of the aviation brigade from Iraq, the battalion was once again complete. Although the brigade was whole again, the CAB did not remain unoccupied. A massive helicopter reset program was initiated, with the battalion still managing to conduct aerial gunnery qualifications, progression flights, continuation flights, and aviation support for the division and other Fort Bragg units. In October Bravo Company took over Operation Bahamas and the Turks and Caicos (OPBAT, a mission of the Drug Enforcement Administration, or DEA) rotations and is currently conducting reconnaissance and air movement

A UH-60 serves as a medical evacuation aircraft during Operation Iraqi Freedom. Medics from the 2nd Battalion, 325th Airborne Infantry Regiment, carry a wounded man to a waiting helicopter bound for Mosul, on the outskirts of Tall Afar, Iraq. *Pfc. James Wilt*

operations in direct support of Drug Enforcement Agency (DEA) operations to interdict the flow of drugs within the Bahamas and the Turks and Caicos Islands.

Now, almost a year after returning to Fort Bragg, and having completed an extensive equipment and aircraft recovery and rebuild, the battalion stands ready to deploy anytime and anywhere within eighteen hours of notification as part of the 82nd Airborne Division and America's strategic first response force. The mission of the 82nd

Combat Aviation Brigade remains that, upon orders, it will deploy worldwide to find, fix, and destroy enemy forces using aerial fire and maneuver to concentrate and sustain combat power.

UH-60 Black Hawk

The mission of the UH-60 is to provide air assault, general support, medical evacuation, command and control, and operational support to the division. The helicopter entered service

Paratroopers watch as a UH-60 Black Hawk helicopter prepares to touch down during the air assault portion of the 82nd Airborne Division's joint forcible entry exercise. *Sgt. Michael Pryor*

with the army in 1979 as a replacement for the aging UH-1 series Bell Huey helicopter as a utility tactical transport helicopter. This versatile Black Hawk has enhanced the overall mobility of the division due to dramatic improvements in troop capacity and cargo lift capability. On the asymmetric battlefield, it provides the commander the agility to get to the fight quicker and to mass effects throughout the battle space across the full spectrum of conflict. An entire fully equipped infantry squad can be lifted in a single Black Hawk and transported faster than in predecessor systems, and in most weather conditions. The Black Hawk can airlift a 105mm howitzer and its crew and transport up to thirty rounds of ammunition in a single lift. The aircraft's critical components and systems are armored or redundant, and its airframe is

A CH-47 Chinook helicopter from Bravo Company, 82nd General Support Aviation Battalion, 4th Brigade Combat Team, sling-loads supplies at the Paruns District Center, in Nuristan province, Afghanistan. *Staff Sgt. Isaac A. Graham*

designed to progressively crush on impact to protect the crew and passengers.

CH-47 Chinook

The Chinook is the largest helicopter in the division's inventory. Its mission is to transport ground forces, supplies, ammunition, and other mission-critical cargo in support of worldwide combat and contingency operations. The large helicopter entered service with the army in 1962 and has proven itself time and time again. Whether in the jungles of Vietnam or the mountains of Afghanistan, the Chinook is the workhorse of the aviation brigade. The CH-47 is a twin-engine, tandem-rotor helicopter that has undergone several iterations and upgrades since the first CH-47A

A U.S. Army CH-47 Chinook helicopter from Combined Joint Task Force 76 flies over the mountains north of Bagram, Afghanistan. The large army helicopters provide insertion, extraction, and resupply of troops in the high altitudes of Afghanistan's mountain ranges. *Staff Sgt. Marcus J. Quarterman*

model was delivered to the army for use in Vietnam. Beginning in 1982 and ending in 1994, all CH-47A, B, and C models were upgraded to the CH-47D version. The D model is currently the U.S. Army standard; it features composite rotor blades, an improved electrical system, modularized hydraulics, triple cargo hooks, avionics and communication improvements, and a more powerful engine that can handle a 19,500-pound load—nearly twice the Chinook's original lift capacity. An upgrade program exists to remanufacture 300 of the current fleet of 425 CH-47Ds to the CH-47F standard.

The Chinook's cockpit accommodates two pilots and an observer. The communications suite includes jam-resistant HF and UHF radio systems, and the helicopter

A tail-gunner keeps a lookout as a CH-47 Chinook helicopter from the General Support Aviation Battalion 3, 82nd Combat Aviation Brigade, takes off at Bagram Air Base, in the Parwan province of Afghanistan. *Staff Sgt. Michael Bracken*

is equipped with an identification friend or foe (IFF) interrogator. Three machine guns can be mounted on the helicopter, two in the crew door on the starboard side and one on the window on the port side. In a defensive mode, the helicopter is equipped with a suite of countermeasure systems that can include one or more of the following: a missile approach warning device, jamming equipment, radar warning devices, and chaff and flare dispensers.

The Chinook has a triple hook system, which provides stability to large external loads or the capacity for multiple external loads. Large external loads such as 155mm howitzers can be transported at speeds up to 260 kilometers per hour using the triple-hook load configuration. Multiple external loads can be delivered to two or three separate destinations in one sortie.

The cabin provides 42 cubic meters of cargo space and 21 square meters of cargo floor area and can accommo-

Members of 1st Battalion, 508th Parachute Infantry Regiment, prepare to deploy as part of Operation Achilles. The aim of the International Security Assistance Force (ISAF) is to help the government of Afghanistan and its institutions develop a stable and prosperous future for the Afghan people. This is achieved by providing security assistance alongside the Afghan National Security Force (ANSF) to enable the extension of good governance, accountability, development, and ultimately, progress. *Corporal Gilyeat (United Kingdom)*

date two HMMWVs, or one HMMWV with a 105mm howitzer and a gun crew. The main cabin can hold up to thirty-three fully equipped troops. When configured for medical evacuation, the cabin can accommodate twenty-four litters.

The Chinook is powered by two T55-GA-714A turboshaft engines, which are pod mounted on either side of the rear pylon under the rear rotor blades. The fuel tanks, which are self sealing, are mounted in external fairings on the sides of the fuselage. The fixed tanks hold 1,030 gallons of fuel. Three additional fuel tanks can be carried in the cargo area.

The CH-47F upgrade program will involve the installation of a new digital cockpit and modifications to the airframe to reduce vibration. The upgraded cockpit will provide future growth potential and will include a digital data bus that permits installation of enhanced communications and navigation equipment for improved situational awareness, mission performance, and survivability. Airframe structural modifications will reduce harmful vibrations, lowering

A CH-47 Chinook helicopter from Bravo Company, 3rd General Support Aviation Battalion, 82nd Combat Aviation Brigade, lands at Forward Operating Base Asadabad, Afghanistan. *Staff Sgt. Isaac A. Graham*

operations and support costs and improving crew endurance. Other airframe modifications will reduce the time required for aircraft teardown and buildup after deployment on a C-5 or C-17 by nearly 60 percent.

The more powerful and reliable T55-GA-714A engines have improved the Chinook's fuel efficiency and enhanced its lift performance by approximately thirty-nine hundred pounds (enabling the Chinook to carry the M198 155mm towed howitzer. Installation of an improved crashworthy extended-range fuel system (ERFS II) will enable Chinook self-deployment and extend the operational radius of all other missions.

OH-58 Kiowa Warrior

The Kiowa Warrior is rapidly deployable by air and can be fully operational within minutes of arrival. Two Kiowa aircraft can be transported in a C-130 aircraft. For air transportation the vertical tail fin pivots, the main rotor blades and the horizontal stabilizer are folded, and the mast-mounted site, the IFF antenna, and the lower wire cutter are removed. And the landing gear can be lowered to decrease the height of the aircraft.

The mission of the OH-58 helicopter is to conduct armed reconnaissance, security, target acquisition and designation, command and control, light attack and defensive

A soldier from Bravo Company, 3rd General Support Aviation Battalion, 82nd Combat Aviation Brigade, remounts his M240B machine gun after offloading mail and supplies at Forward Operating Base Kalagush, in Nuristan province, Afghanistan. *Staff Sgt. Isaac Graham*

Sgt. Michael Gurley, flight engineer for Company B, 3rd General Support Aviation Battalion, 82nd Combat Aviation Brigade, scans the terrain for activity from the opening of a CH-47 Chinook. *Pfc. Aubree Rundle*

Sgt. 1st Class Jerry Eaton, maintenance platoon sergeant, 1st Squadron, 17th Cavalry, Task Force Liberty Iraq, replaces a part on the foot of an OH-58D Kiowa at Forward Operating Base MacKenzie, Iraq. *Staff Sgt. Matthew Acosta*

An OH-58 Kiowa helicopter takes on fuel at a forward arming and refueling point. Note the pilot's M4 carbine through the front windscreen, as well as a few personal items to remind him of home. *Staff Sgt. Matthew Acosta*

air combat missions in support of combat, and contingency operations. The Kiowa Warrior replaced the AH-1 Cobra attack helicopter, which had functioned as scouts in air cavalry troops and light attack companies. Entering service with the army in 1991, the Kiowa is a single-engine, four-bladed helicopter with advanced navigation, communication, and weapons and cockpit integration systems.

The mast-mounted sight (MMS) houses a thermal imaging system, a low-light television, a laser range finder/designator, and an optical bore sight system. These systems enable the Kiowa Warrior to operate in both day and night environments and allow target acquisition and engagement at standoff ranges and in adverse weather conditions. The highly accurate navigation system of the OH-58 provides precise target location that can be sent digitally to other aircraft or artillery via an advanced digital communications system. Battlefield imagery can also be transmitted to provide near-real-time situational awareness to command-and-control elements. The laser designator can provide autonomous designation for the laser-guided Hellfire or remote designation for other laser-guided precision weapons.

The Kiowa Warrior is equipped with two universal quick-change weapons pylons. Each pylon can be armed with two Hellfire missiles, seven Hydra-70 rockets, two air-to-air Stinger missiles, or one .50-caliber fixed-forward machine gun. The armament systems combine to provide antiarmor, antipersonnel, and antiaircraft capabilities at standoff ranges.

Kiowas and Pink Teams

Operating out of FOB MacKenzie, OH-58 Kiowa Warrior helicopters are engaged in continuously developing combat and combat support tactics in an effort to fight the enemy insurgents in Iraq. Helicopter patrols called "Pink Teams" are being implemented to maximize the effectiveness of two very different helicopter platforms, backing maximum

Sgt. John Ryan, armament sergeant, 1st Squadron, 17th Cavalry, Task Force Liberty, Iraq, checks the headspace on the .50-caliber machine gun mounted on an OH-58D Kiowa helicopter. *Staff Sgt. Matthew Acosta*

Helicopters of the 1st Squadron, 17th Cavalry, Task Force Liberty, Iraq. Helicopter patrols known as Pink Teams are being implemented to maximize the effectiveness of two very different helicopter platforms. The teams include the OH-58 Kiowa as the scout and the AH-64 Apache as the hunter. This rotary combination provides maximum observational capabilities with increased firepower. *Staff Sgt. Matthew Acosta*

Spc. Andrew Heath, fuel specialist, 1st Squadron, 17th Cavalry, Task Force Liberty, loads a rocket pod on an OH-58D Kiowa helicopter prior to a combined patrol with an AH-64D Apache. *Staff Sgt. Matthew Acosta*

A U.S. Army AH-64D Apache Longbow helicopter loaded for bear is a welcome sight for any U.S. ground pounder, and a nightmare for the Taliban. This helicopter is armed with 30mm chain cannon, eight AGM-114 Hellfire air-to-ground missiles, and two rocket pods each holding nineteen 2.75-inch rockets. *Master Sgt. Lance Cheung, U.S. Air Force*

observational capabilities with increased firepower. The Pink Team concept originated during the Vietnam War when smaller OH-6 Cayuse (also called "Loach") scout helicopters were paired with AH-1 Cobra gunships. These teams worked in tandem to find, fix, and destroy enemy troops.

Today Pink Teams consist of an OH-58D Kiowa reconnaissance helicopter and an AH-64A Apache attack helicopter. Although the aircraft were developed for different roles, the helicopter crews of both aircraft were able to effectively communicate and have adapted to the other aircraft's flying capabilities after a brief training program. Capt. Andrew Cecil, commander, Company B, 8th Battalion, 229th Aviation Brigade, Task Force Liberty, related, "We initiated a short training program integrating both aircraft, getting the pilots used to patrolling with each other. Obviously, they're different aircraft with different

abilities, so we came up with a plan on how to get the best from both platforms."

Since the Pink Team doctrine was initiated, observational capabilities and technology have come a long way. With the assistance of night and heat-sensing imaging, the helicopters have an advantage over the enemy. According to Chief Warrant Officer 2 Steven Hamm, pilot, Troop B, 1-17 Cavalry, "In today's scout aircraft, the eye can be rotated around 320 degrees, and has night vision and thermal imaging capabilities allowing it to see in adverse weather conditions. It also has a thirty-two-power zoom so it can bring things in really close for standing off a target." Hamm continues, "The system also has the capability to take photos of an area or target and send them through a satellite link back to the headquarters if needed. Due to the OH-58D Kiowa's smaller size, it's much more nimble

Spc. Michael Clark prepares to load 30mm rounds into an AH-64D Apache Longbow helicopter at Forward Operating Base Salerno, in the Khowst province of Afghanistan. Clark is from Bravo Company, 122nd Support Aviation Battalion, 82nd Combat Aviation Brigade. *Staff Sgt. Isaac A. Graham*

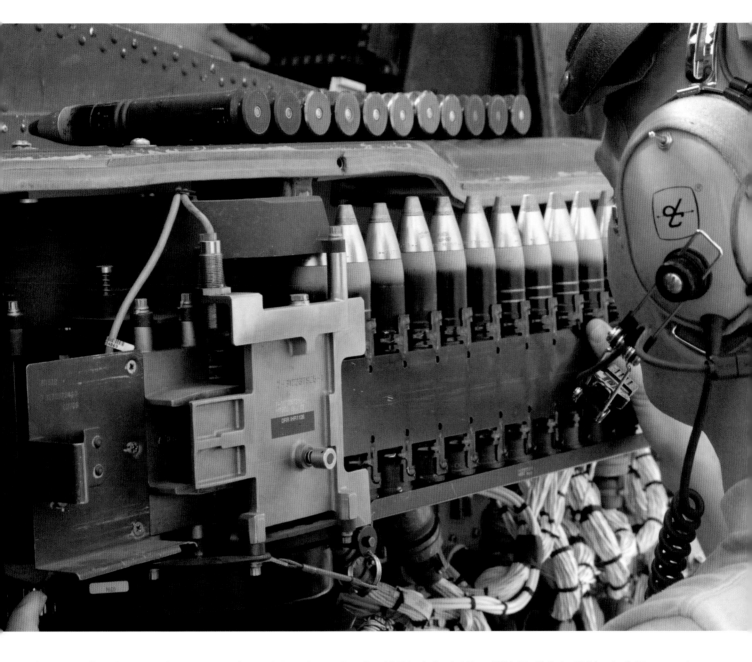

Spc. Michael Clark, from Bravo Company, 122nd Support Aviation Support Battalion, 4th Brigade Combat Team (BCT), 82nd Infantry Division, loads 30mm rounds into an AH-64D Longbow Apache helicopter at Forward Operating Base Salerno, Khowst province, Afghanistan. *Staff Sgt. Isaac A. Graham*

than the larger gunship and has a very wide, unobstructed view around the aircraft."

Chief Warrant Officer 2 James Williamson, pilot, Troop D, 1st Squadron, 17th Cavalry, Task Force Liberty commented, "A drawback of the small scout helicopter is its limited ability to lift weight in armament. Its relatively light weapons systems, typically a .50-caliber machine gun and a seven-rocket pod, are primarily for self-defense, but are often used to assist coalition ground forces when needed. This is a reconnaissance bird, not an attack helicopter, but we can lay down fire for soldiers in trouble on the ground.

"On the other hand," continued Williamson, "the Apache has exceptional firepower. The Apache AH-64A is equipped with a 30mm cannon with up to twelve hundred rounds and precision laser aiming. It can carry up to sixteen laser-guided Hellfire missiles or four rocket

A Hellfire missile hangs mounted on an AH-64D Apache Longbow helicopter at Forward Operating Base Salerno, in the Khowst province of Afghanistan. *Staff Sgt. Isaac A. Graham*

pods with nineteen rockets in each pod, or a combination, depending on the mission. Together, these teams have the capability to handle any mission needed to counter any enemy attack here in Iraq."

Because the scouts are able to fly lower than the Apache, they can relay target information and location to the larger, higher-flying helicopter, which can then home in and defeat or destroy the target. The first time the Pink Team came into contact with the enemy, the 1st Battalion, 15th Infantry soldiers were pinned down and the Kiowa was able to direct fire where the soldiers said they wanted it; the team was able to stay on site for almost an hour engaging the enemy. If this had been a typical dual OH-58D combo, the pilots would have expended all their ordnance and would have had to return to base to reload. Integrating the two helicopters from two units into a single team has proven to be a success to the U.S. and coalition soldiers.

Commenting on the use of the two-helicopter platforms, Lt. Col. Frank Muth, commander, 1/17 Cavalry, said, "It's a great concept utilizing the available technology we have here by combining the fighting force of two units with a common mission either supporting the ground forces or direct contact with the enemy during the Pink Team patrols." Muth reported that since the teams have been implemented, the missions had been going so well that he didn't foresee returning to the dual-scout combination unless a specific mission mandated it. "Combining the abilities of two very different aircraft makes for an unstoppable team."

AH-64D Apache Longbow

The AH-64 Apache is the army's heavy division/corps attack helicopter. The AH-64D Longbow remanufacture effort incorporates a millimeter wave fire control radar (FCR), radar frequency interferometer (RFI), fire-and-forget radar-guided Hellfire missile, and cockpit management and digitization enhancements. The combination of the FCR, RFI, and the advanced navigation and avionics suite of the aircraft provides increased situational awareness, lethality, and survivability. The

The AH-64D Apache Longbow is the U.S. Army's premiere helicopter gunship, providing close air support to the paratroopers as they hunt down the Taliban or Iraqi insurgents. *Master Sgt. Lance Cheung, U.S. Air Force*

mission of the AH-64D is to conduct rear, close, and deep precision strike missions. The helicopter can also be tasked to provide armed reconnaissance when required in day and night environments, on obscured battlefields, and in adverse weather conditions. The Longbow has a crew of two—a pilot and a co-pilot/gunner. The aircraft is armed with AGM-114 Hellfire missiles, 2.75-inch folding-fin rockets, and a M230 30mm chain gun.

Soldiers with the 2nd Assault Helicopter Battalion (AHB), 82nd Combat Aviation Brigade, 82nd Airborne Division, and the British Royal Air Force's 51st Squadron trained together near Kandahar Airfield, Afghanistan, to increase the soldiers' confidence in utilizing Apache support in their battle rhythm. As ground troops trained to repel an insurgent attack at Tarnak Farms Range in Kandahar province, the call was made for AH-64D Apache Longbow helicopter support. "Arrow 26" answered the call, arriving on station amidst simulated small-arms fire and smoke marking friendly positions. Commented fire support officer Capt. Andrew Ruszkiewicz, "There is no doubt that the AH-64D helicopter is intimidating with its weapons system on the battlefield. This is true not only for enemy forces but also to the friendly forces not familiar in conducting close combat attacks."

Chapter 6

GLOBAL WAR ON TERRORISM

A soldier from A Company, 2nd Battalion, 504th Parachute Infantry Regiment, White Devils, sights through his 5.56mm M4 carbine rifle during a combat patrol in the mountains of Adi Ghar, Afghanistan, in support of Operation Enduring Freedom. *Staff Sgt. Leopold Medina, Jr.*

Following the attack on the United States on September 11, 2001, President George W. Bush called upon the might of the American military to fight global terrorism. Their marching orders from the commander in chief were to bring the terrorists to justice or justice to the terrorists. In support of the global war on terrorism (GWOT), the paratroopers of the 82nd Airborne Division would be deployed to Afghanistan and the Central Command (CENTCOM) area of responsibility (AOR) to support combat operations.

In June 2002 the 82nd Airborne's Task Force Panther, made up of elements from the 505th Parachute Infantry Regiment and other 82nd units, deployed to Afghanistan in support of Operation Enduring Freedom (OEF). Task Force Devil, made up of the 504th PIR and other 82nd elements, replaced Task Force Panther in January 2003.

Operation Enduring Freedom

Paratroopers of the 82nd Airborne Division moved across the desert wasteland of Forward Operating Base (FOB) Warrior and loaded onto a waiting CH-47 Chinook helicopter. These soldiers were part of Task Force Fury working with the Afghan National Army (ANA) soldiers in Operation Andar Fury. The operation was a six-day

Paratroopers from B Company, 1st Battalion, 508th Parachute Infantry Regiment, 4th Brigade Combat Team, move out on patrol into the Ghorak Valley of Helmand province, in southern Afghanistan, during Operation Achilles. *Sgt. Tony J. Spain*

mission of U.S. and ANA forces into the Ghazni province. The combined force introduced a company-size force into the Ebrahim Khel area, which previously had not seen a large presence of U.S. or coalition forces. According to 1st Lt. Ernest Orlando, executive officer for Company B, 2nd Battalion, 508th Parachute Infantry Regiment, 82nd Airborne Division, who led the mission, "That was one of the main goals of the mission, to demonstrate coalition presence in the area." Company A, 2/508 PIR, ANA forces, and various other attached soldiers also participated in the mission.

The paratroopers started their mission late in the evening. After dismounting from the relative safety of their armored Humvees, the paratroopers walked approximately twelve "klicks" to the outskirts of Ebrahim Khel. In their rucksacks, they carried their combat supplies plus a two-day supply of food and water. From that point on, the mission

Paratroopers from Company F, 2nd Battalion, 508th Parachute Infantry Regiment, 4th Brigade Combat Team, conduct a dismounted patrol during a combat logistics convoy near Firebase Miri, in eastern Afghanistan. *Pfc. Micah Clare*

Paratroopers of the 82nd Airborne Division patrol the mountains of Afghanistan during Operation Enduring Freedom. As the dismounted patrol maneuvers across the hazardous terrain, their teammates provide security in the HMMWVs on the road below. The terrain clearly affords an advantage to the enemy forces, who hold the high ground. The soldier on the right is armed with an enhanced battle rifle with an ACOG scope. *82nd Airborne Division Public Affairs Office*

would be conducted without the assistance of additional ground support. Any means of resupply would be provided from aircraft dropping it to the soldiers on the ground. Although this was the first time the mission was carried out in this manner, it allowed the unit to be mobile, and rapid in its movements.

One of the paratroopers, Spc. Matthew Steffen, an M249 squad automatic weapon gunner with Company B, related, "I think we went back to the basics. Good old hardcore, light infantry tactics. No vehicles, just pursuing the enemy on foot. If we had gone in by vehicle, the Taliban forces would have heard us coming and been prepared."

Over the following days, the paratroopers entered the villages in the area during the day, talking to the local Afghans and searching for any sign of the Taliban presence. At night, the units typically moved one to two miles and set up in a different area.

With several units maneuvering around in this manner, acting as separate elements, the U.S. and ANA forces were able to establish a greater presence in the area. 1st Lt. Brian Kitching, a platoon leader with Company B, commented, "The Taliban were not able to predict what we would do next. We wanted to clear the area of operations in order to disrupt Taliban activity and by our presence we flushed them out."

On this operation the paratroopers along with the ANA allies located a weapons cache of two AK-47 rifles, one rocket-propelled grenade launcher, three antiarmor rocket-propelled grenades (RPGs), two antipersonnel mines, and a medical cache. Kitching related, "I think it went extremely well, and we're still processing all the information."

By demonstrating a presence of coalition and ANA forces, the mission also allowed the leaders of both forces to meet with the local populace and establish a line of trust and cooperation. "The villagers were initially wary of us, but after spending forty-eight hours there they were very receptive," Orlando said.

Commented Kitching, "The acceptance of coalition forces by the villagers and the successful completion of the mission were both aided by the support of the ANA. The assets they bring to us are knowledge of the local populace and terrain. I enjoyed working with them. They have an extreme dedication to their country and are always working toward the betterment of Afghanistan."

Having the opportunity to actually see the villages, the paratroopers themselves gleaned a better appreciation for the overall mission in Afghanistan and the importance of it. Specialist Steffen related a conversation with one of

A convoy of HMMWVs from the 82nd Airborne Division travels across the barren wilderness of Afghanistan. The vast mountain ranges serve as a hiding ground for the elusive al Qaeda forces. The weather and terrain provide a challenge to the American and coalition soldiers as they pursue the enemy in Operation Enduring Freedom. *82nd Airborne Division Public Affairs Office*

Paratroopers of the 82nd Airborne Division man a security stop along a desolate Afghanistan highway. The soldiers are armed with M4A1 carbines; the trooper in the HMMWV mans an M2 .50-caliber machine gun. On the rear deck are cases of MREs; the deck offers a good view of smoke grenade launchers. *82nd Airborne Division Public Affairs Office*

the old men of the village who told him that the Taliban took all of his food and beat him. Steffen said, "We were burning in the heat from all the gear and we were tired, but it was worth it. We are winning here, but it's not a war you can really measure. We know it's important to help give Afghanistan back to its people for their future."

After six days in the field, the paratroopers climbed aboard their CH-47 helicopters and returned to FOB Warrior. Their relief at returning to base and refitting for future missions was coupled with the sense that they actually had made a difference in the lives of the average Afghan.

Operation Achilles

At the request of the Islamic Republic of Afghanistan's government, soldiers from NATO's Iraqi Security Assistance Force (ISAF) and the Afghan National Security Force (ANSF) launched a major operation targeting Taliban and drug traffickers in southern Afghanistan. According to Dutch major general Ton Van Loon, commander, Regional Command South, "Operations will focus on improving security in areas where Taliban extremists, foreign terrorists, and [narcotics] traffickers are trying to destabilize the

government of Afghanistan. We also intend to empower village elders to take charge of their communities as they have been doing in other parts of southern Afghanistan, without the influence of Taliban extremists."

Codenamed Operation Achilles, the multinational force operating in the northern region of the Helmand province involved more than five thousand soldiers, including one thousand from the Afghan National Security Force and nearly a thousand paratroopers from the 1st Battalion, 508th Parachute Infantry Regiment, 4th Brigade Combat Team, 82nd Airborne Division.

The primary responsibility for the operation was under the command of the British, with the 1st Battalion, 508th Parachute Infantry Regiment, 4th Brigade Combat Team, 82nd Airborne Division, providing support to assist in isolating and preventing the Taliban from escaping. The paratroopers also coordinated a convoy and night air assault in the Ghorak Valley of the Helmand province. Operation Achilles was one of the largest multinational combined ANSF and ISAF missions launched in Afghanistan. Although the operation focused on improving security conditions, its overarching purpose was to assist the govern-

Staff Sgt. Michael Robinson, a squad leader with Company B, 2nd Battalion, 508th Parachute Infantry Regiment, 4th Brigade Combat Team, and Afghan National Army (ANA) forces search the house of a suspected Taliban militant. Robinson and his unit conducted the joint mission with ANA forces in the Ghazni province of Afghanistan. *Spc. Matthew Leary*

ment of Afghanistan in improving its ability to begin reconstruction and economic development in the area.

Commented Maj. Gen. Ton Van Loon, "Strategically, our goal is to enable the Afghan government to begin the Kajaki Project. The Kajaki multipurpose dam and power house will improve the water supply for local communities, rehabilitate irrigation systems for farmlands, as well as provide sufficient electrical power for residents, industries, and commerce."

During the second day of operations, ANSF soldiers captured a high-ranking Taliban commander and suicide-bomb attack facilitator. This commander, Mullah Mahmood, was arrested at an ANSF checkpoint as he tried to escape dressed in a burka, a veil worn by Islamic woman there.

General Van Loon remarked, "The capture of this senior Taliban extremist is another indicator that a more normal life is returning to the Zahre and Panjwaii districts, and is a testament to the great work the ANA is achieving. This type of security crackdown in Panjwaii is an example of the ultimate goals of Operation Achilles. With stability provided by the ANA, much needed reconstruction will commence for the people of southern Afghanistan."

Operation Nowruz Jhala

Operation Nowruz Jhala was an ANA-led mission whose aim was to hunt down Taliban, al Qaeda, and other criminal elements in Kapisa, a province in eastern Afghanistan long known for its lawlessness. The coalition and the Afghan

Another day comes to a close as the sun sets a world away from Fort Bragg, North Carolina. A gunner in 3rd Platoon, Troop Bravo, 4th Squadron, 73rd Cavalry Regiment, 4th Brigade Combat Team, pulls evening guard after his platoon has set up a patrol base for the night in Paktika province, Afghanistan. *Pfc. Micah Clare*

As the day turns into night, paratroopers of the 82nd Airborne head into the mountains on patrol in pursuit of the enemy. The al Qaeda forces may be more familiar with the terrain, but the American soldiers are equipped with night-vision equipment and tenacity. And they can call in the division's Apache helicopter gunships as well as other coalition aircraft to support their missions. *82nd Airborne Division Public Affairs Office*

forces had given the area a wide berth after the initial invasion in 2001. This would be the first time that the ANA and the coalition would be going into the valley with a sizable force with plans to remain in the area until the Taliban was completely removed. Elements of the Afghan National Army, Afghan National Police (ANP), and U.S. forces swept into a Taliban stronghold in Kapisa.

The ANA, the vanguard unit during this operation, led the charge into the valleys surrounding Tagab. Following them was the ANP and coalition forces from the 82nd Airborne Division. The ANP were used to search homes in the villages, question people, then provide a permanent presence for security; coalition forces were to provide additional firepower, command and control, and mentorship while in the field.

According to 1st Lt. Dennis L. Chamberlain, detachment commander, 82nd Division Special Troops Battalion, "We [the 82nd] are basically the Afghan's maneuver element, making sure they don't get in over their heads. We have a much better ability to have overall situational awareness of the entire battlefield. So far the mission has been successful, netting many high valued Taliban targets and killing many more during fierce fights in some of the more remote areas of the province."

During a mission into Ala Sai Valley, U.S. and Afghan fighters ambushed Taliban forces three separate times as they exited the valley. Maj. Bill Myer, police mentor from the Michigan National Guard and part of U.S. Task Force Phoenix and the Combined Security Transition Command-Afghanistan, remarked, "The fighting was intense. One firefight lasted close to forty minutes. We [the ANP] were engaging the insurgents with rocket-propelled grenades, small arms and our crew-served weapons. Finally, we had to call in artillery and close air support." After the close air support ended, the Taliban's guns fell silent and the Afghan and U.S. forces were able to leave Ala Sai Valley without further incident. No U.S., ANA, or ANP forces were killed or wounded during these ambushes.

Two days later, the Afghan security forces and U.S. forces traveled back to the Ala Sai Valley with reinforcements with the purpose of tracking down insurgents and eliminating the threat they posed to the civilian populace. This time the ANSF and coalition forces did not encounter

Paratroopers from Company C, 3rd Battalion, 325th Airborne Infantry Regiment, line up against the wall of a compound they are preparing to raid during an operation in Baghdad. The paratroopers wait in a stack for the signal to dash across the street and raid a compound suspected of harboring insurgents. The cordon-and-knock operation targeted suspected insurgent safe houses. *Sgt. Michael Pryor*

heavy resistance, rather only sporadic small-arms fire and RPGs fired at their forces. Major Myer reported, "We were able to accomplish the mission traveling to the end of the dirt road in the valley. This time the police searched every home in the villages we came upon, finding some contraband and gathering important intelligence for future missions."

The final village at the end of the Ala Sai Valley involved a significant challenge for the Americans. The road crumbled under the weight of a Humvee and almost caused it to roll over. The local Afghans came to the aid of the U.S. forces, shoring up the road and preventing the Humvee from rolling over. "After extracting the Humvee and talking to the villagers, we found out we were the first Americans they had ever encountered," Myer remarked. "In fact the last foreigners they had seen were Russians. We talked with the village elders and they were a little apprehensive. Apparently, the Taliban had told the villagers [that] Americans would not let any of the Afghans who worked for them to pray. The police commander and my interpreter quickly dispelled this. It really is about gaining the trust of the Afghans and I think we accomplished this."

73rd Cavalry Regiment Supports Operation Enduring Freedom

One of the 82nd Airborne Division news units is the 4th Battalion of the 73rd Cavalry (4/73), which stood up on

A U.S. Army HMMWV parks at the entrance of Saddam Hussein's former palace. Now called Camp Prosperity, it is the new home of Charlie and Delta companies, 3rd Battalion, 325th Airborne Infantry Regiment, 82nd Airborne Division. Nothing but the best accommodations for the paratroopers of the 82nd—hooah! *Sgt. Michael Pryor*

22 June 2006. To be a soldier in today's army, it is a safe bet you are going to train hard, learn the lessons of those who have gone before you, deploy downrange, and fight. According to Command Sgt. Maj. Michael Green, 4/73 Cav, 82nd Airborne Division, "As we stood up and have gone from just a few soldiers to actually deploying as a whole unit, our strength has been our platoon sergeants. They were able to proficiently integrate, train, and educate all of these new soldiers, many of whom have never been in the 82nd before. They didn't really have any experience, and integrating them into the squads and platoons was a challenge in and of itself. I can't stress enough how the senior NCOs were the glue that held this unit together."

Not only had many of the soldiers never dealt with the legendary 82nd Airborne Division, nearly all of the lower enlisted troops came straight from advanced individual training (AIT). "Being in the [4/73 Cav] has definitely been a leadership challenge if ever I have seen one," said 1st Sgt. Paul Correale, Headquarters and Headquarters Troop. "Our [noncommissioned officers] have definitely kept this unit together."

According to Green, "A unit typically gets a year to eighteen months together to train and work out standard operating procedures. We haven't had that much time, and getting our people trained on vital battle drills was a big challenge. A lot of the training is muscle memory. Once soldiers learn how to do their tasks, it's automatic. Prior to going to the Joint Readiness Training Center (JRTC), Fort Polk, Louisiana, the unit was not ready. JRTC helped to refine the soldier's skill and better prepare them for Afghanistan."

Not long after members of the regiment went to JRTC to validate their training, they were deployed. The 4/73 Cav hit the ground running around 15 January 2007 and never looked back. The regiment's main area of operation is in the western part of the Paktika province. Because of the mobility of the cavalry, it is able to control and cover a larger AO than would normally be expected.

Since arriving in Afghanistan, Green has lived through many experiences that made him proud to lead this unit. "There have been quite a few proud moments for me, but the best so far has got to be when we executed and completed our first operation. The operation was planned and executed impressively from the squad up to the squadron level. The platoons and troops hit the objectives just as they were supposed to and everything went just as planned." The soldiers of the 4/73 Cav continued to work closely with the ANA and ANSF to make the country safe, separate the enemy from the population, and give the population a chance to grow.

Operation Warrior Sweep

In its previous operations in the Ayubkhel Valley in Afghanistan, the 82nd Airborne Division had conducted many village searches, but the fourth day of the division's participation in Operation Warrior Sweep proved to be the most successful one yet. A day after the elements of the 2/505 and 2/504 infantry regiments, 82nd Airborne Division, endured a six-mile march through rugged mountains and high altitudes, the infantry soldiers prepared to search a village for any signs of Taliban and al Qaeda fighters.

Working in squads, the paratroopers methodically searched the houses of the first major village they encountered during the operation. The 3rd Squad, 3rd Platoon, Company B, 2nd Battalion, 505th Infantry Regiment, quickly uncovered a weapons cache of grenades, blocks of C-4 plastic explosives, and various types of ammunition in a locked storage room of one house.

"This wasn't too different from our other missions," said Staff Sgt. Brandon Gass, 2nd Squad leader, Company B, 2/505 Infantry Regiment, 82nd Airborne Division. "We've cleared villages four times since we've been in country. We've been out a couple times and haven't found anything, but finding stuff gets everyone's adrenaline going and it makes the operation a whole lot more exciting."

Continuing on their patrol, 2nd Squad, 3rd Platoon, Company B, 2/505 Infantry Regiment, uncovered in another house an old Russian military two-way radio, a fifty-pound crate of dynamite, a rocket-propelled grenade round, a box of antiaircraft rounds, and hundreds of 7.62mm and handgun rounds. Sgt. Nick Cameron, 2nd Squad, Company B, 2/505 Infantry Regiment, reported that the local children actually helped his squad find a large ammunition cache. "When we went to the house that we actually found the bad stuff in, the kids knew nothing about it but they were more than willing to help us with everything," Other paratroopers discovered additional caches and added to the list of confiscated ammunitions and explosives: twenty RPGs, dozens of grenades, and scores of small-arms ammunition. The cache was later destroyed by an engineer team from 3rd Platoon, 307th Engineer Battalion, 82nd Airborne Division.

According to 2nd Lt. Che Atkinson, 3rd Platoon leader, Company B, 2/505 Infantry Regiment, despite finding a stockpile of ammunition and explosives in the village, no military rifles or weapon firing systems were found. "We believe the enemy forces may have known ahead of time about the soldiers' coming. The [Taliban and al Qaeda] personnel knew we were coming so they packed up what weapons they could, but they left a lot of stuff behind. The more stuff we find, the less stuff they have to come back to."

Along with finding the ammunition caches, the soldiers also took six local nationals into custody for further questioning at Bagram Air Base. The six persons under control (PUCs) were taken into custody based on assessments made by the

U.S. Army soldiers breach a house to search for insurgent activities during an operation in Zaghiniyat, Iraq. The mission is to rid an area of insurgent forces and allow coalition forces freedom of movement throughout the area of operations. The soldiers are with Charlie Troop, 5th Squadron, 73rd Cavalry Regiment, 82nd Airborne Division. *Staff Sgt. Joann Makinano*

Paratroopers from Company C, 2nd Battalion, 325th Airborne Infantry Regiment, Task Force White Falcon, conduct presence patrols in Tall Afar, Iraq. Patrolling through the neighborhoods, the soldiers make an effort to be seen by the local people and the local insurgents. *Pfc. James Wilt*

military interrogation team on site or because ammunition or explosives were found in their homes. Dealing with the local population proved to be a demanding task for soldiers because the enemy can easily blend in with the local populace.

Although there was no contact with anticoalition or antigovernment forces, the 82nd Airborne Division's role in Operation Warrior Sweep was a great success, according to 1st Sgt. LaMarquis Knowles, Company B, 2/505 Infantry Regiment. "This has been the most successful mission we've been on, based on the fact that we've recovered so much ammunition and explosives, this culminates everything."

Operation Iraqi Freedom

In February 2003 the 2nd Brigade Combat Team (BCT) deployed, along with the division headquarters, to Kuwait in support of Operation Iraqi Freedom (OIF). The division conducted sustained combat operations throughout Iraq and the CENTCOM area of operations. In May 2003 the division headquarters returned to Fort Bragg, North Carolina. The 2nd BCT remained in Iraq attached to the 1st Armored Division and continued to conduct combat operations. The division headquarters, along with the 3rd BCT and elements of the division artillery, communication, aviation, and separate battalions returned to Iraq in August 2003 to continue command and control over combat operations in and around Baghdad.

In January 2004 the 1st BCT deployed to Iraq to conduct combat operations in OIF. The 2nd BCT redeployed to Fort Bragg in February. The division headquarters was relieved by the 1st Marine Expeditionary Division in March 2004, and the remaining 82nd forces in Iraq redeployed to Fort Bragg by the end of April 2004. In September 2004 the 82nd's Division Ready Force (DRF-1), 1/505, was deployed to support OEF 6 in support of Joint Task Force 76 (JTF 76) and the Afghanistan elections. In December 2004 the 82nd's 1/17 Cav, Task Force (TF) 2/325 and TF 3/325, deployed to Iraq in support of the Iraqi national elections.

82nd Airborne in Baghdad

The paratroopers from the 2nd "Falcon" Brigade, which had been based in Kuwait as a ready reserve, were sent to Baghdad, Iraq's capital city, in January 2007. There the paratroopers were to be followed over the next several months by four more combat brigades, strengthening U.S. forces by approximately twenty thousand soldiers. The increase in troops was an effort to help clamp down on violence in the city and pave the way for the Iraqi government to assume full control of Baghdad's security.

The 2nd BCT was organized under the Multi-National Division-Baghdad, headed by the 1st Cavalry Division. The brigade conducted operations in conjunction with the Iraqi Security Forces (ISF). As part of their mission, the Falcons sent paratroopers into some of Baghdad's most volatile areas to pursue a "clear, hold, and build" strategy against insurgents.

According to the brigade's operations sergeant major John Bagby, "Our mission will be to secure our area of operation, hold that area, and then, at a said time, to turn that area over to the ISF. The paratroopers' special training and ability to adapt to changing circumstances make them uniquely suited to overcome the obstacles of counter-insurgency warfare. They can turn on a dime if necessary, change missions, and still go out and execute. There is no doubt in my mind that paratroopers from the Falcon Brigade are ready to go out into sector and take the fight to the enemy."

The Falcon Brigade is one of the most combat-experienced units in the army. Paratroopers from the 2nd BCT have deployed six times on short notice since the global war on terrorism began. Many of the paratroopers are on their third or fourth tour of duty in Iraq. One of

Taking back the streets, the "Black Falcons" put boots on the ground in Iraq. Staff Sgt. Steven Michaelis, a squad leader from Battery B, 2nd Battalion, 319th Airborne Field Artillery Regiment, 2nd Brigade Combat Team, takes the point as his platoon moves down a street in Adhamiyah. *Sgt. Michael Pryor*

the 2nd BCT's battalions returned from a deployment in December 2006, having spent only weeks at home before being redeployed to Kuwait.

Captain Priscilla Smoot, commander of Company A, 407th Brigade Support Battalion, related, "Our soldiers are willing to do whatever we ask them to do. Paratroopers in the 82nd have always had that attitude." Staff Sgt. Jack Butler, a platoon sergeant with Company C, 1st Battalion, 504th Parachute Infantry Regiment, echoed those sentiments, "The Falcons arrived in Baghdad trained, equipped, and ready to fight. Now that they've put boots on the ground, it will be up to the young paratroopers and junior noncommissioned officers to make sure the mission gets completed. Whatever they put out in front of us, we're going to be able to tackle."

Making Its Presence Known

Every day, paratroopers from Company C, 2nd Battalion, 325th Airborne Infantry Regiment, 82nd Airborne Division, conduct presence patrols throughout the neighborhoods in Tall Afar, Iraq, in an effort to be seen by the local people and the local insurgents. As they had done countless times before, the paratroopers head out on their patrol. Staff Sgt. Haven Crecelius, an infantryman, commented, "The people see the paratroopers on the street. The residents often approach the soldiers to speak to them. But, the insurgents also see the paratroopers on the street and on more than one occasion have attacked them. Insurgent attacks against the paratroopers, while dangerous, play into the hands of the soldiers. In our minds it is a movement to contact; we're trying to draw the insurgents out, so that we can take them down."

Sgt. 1st Class Robert Farnsworth, a platoon sergeant with Company A, 325th Special Troops Battalion, 2nd Brigade Combat Team, pulls security next to a soldier from the 3rd Battalion, 2nd Brigade, 6th Iraqi Army Division, during a morning clearing operation in Baghdad's Adhamiyah district. *Sgt. Michael Pryor*

The morning air is crisp, cool, and quiet as the patrol proceeds along its route of travel. Then all of a sudden the calm is broken as a single shot rings out. Reacting to the incoming fire, the paratroopers break for cover and search for the shooter. As the soldiers scan the buildings for the insurgent, they perform a bounding overwatch maneuver toward the area where the shot is believed to have come from. Crecelius reports, "Even though the paratroopers conduct presence patrols at least twice a day, the men rarely come under fire. We don't usually take contact; it's just been a few separate times. We move on shots; wherever shots come from we move to them to try to get to the shooter."

Although moving through the city on foot makes the men of Company C targets, they feel that being dismounted is to their advantage. Crecelius commented, "We can maneuver better on the ground than in vehicles. Vehicles can get somewhere quicker

and cordon off an area, but dismounted we can maneuver, take cover, and locate the shooter better than the vehicle can."

Even though they are a dismounted unit, the soldiers still depend on vehicles. Spc. Scott Johnson, an infantryman, explained, "If we get contact, we have vehicle support; we have to do this because besides informants this is the only way we can identify exactly who is bad or an area they are operating."

The paratroopers also realize the impact their presence has on the inhabitants of the city. As activity has increased, the locals see the paratroopers still on the streets even though it's been getting heated again. The people know that the soldiers are not going to leave and will finish what they started.

Operation Clean Sweep

Soldiers from the Iraqi Army (IA) and paratroopers from Company D, 2nd Battalion, 505th Parachute Infantry

Spc. Martin Garza, an artilleryman with Battery B, 2nd Battalion, 319th Airborne Field Artillery Regiment, 2nd Brigade Combat Team, and a fellow paratrooper patrol Adhamiyah, Iraq, which is known as a hot spot for improvised explosive devices (IEDs). Using cover and concealment, the pair of troopers keep a watchful eye out for insurgents. *Sgt. Michael Pryor*

Regiment, 82nd Airborne Division, with support from helicopters from 1st Battalion, 150th Aviation Regiment, West Virginia Army National Guard, attached to the 2nd Battalion, 25th Aviation Regiment, and 25th Combat Aviation Brigade landed in Tikrit, in northern Iraq. As they exited the UH-60 Black Hawk helicopters, the soldiers hit the ground and set up a defense perimeter even before the dust, rocks, and debris stirred up by the helicopter settled back to the ground.

Their mission was to locate and destroy a suspected insurgent training site. According to Sgt. 1st Class Chad Eske, the platoon sergeant with 3rd Platoon, Company D, 2/505 PIR, 82nd Airborne Division, "It's a joint mission with IA soldiers checking out a possible cache. Basically whatever we find we'll blow in place and do some tactical

questioning with residents in the area." The mission, dubbed Operation Clean Sweep, was in response to a report of a suspicious area seen by aircrew members as they flew missions overhead. It was reported that the site was littered with piles of empty ammunitions tubes and boxes, so the paratroopers were sent in to check it out.

Once on the ground, the soldiers verified the reports as accurate. The Iraqi and coalition soldiers ultimately discovered an apparent insurgent training site complete with mortar tubes, rocket-propelled grenade launchers, blank ammunition rounds, and training boards with diagrams explaining how to use various weapons. The cache had been located in and around a small group of brick-and-mud buildings near the landing site.

This paratrooper of the 82nd Airborne Division is ready for battle. The American soldier is the best trained and equipped solider in the world. He carries on the tradition of those who have gone before who earned the title Devils in Baggy Pants. When their country calls, the men and women of the 82nd Airborne answer the call. They are and remain America's Guard of Honor. *82nd Airborne Division Public Affairs Office*

Along on the mission with the IA and paratroopers was a special soldier, a dog named Eddie. The dog explored the site, hunting diligently for any additional ammunition or explosives. Staff Sgt. Jason L. Robbins, Eddie's trainer, followed the canine closely, directing and rewarding his four-footed teammate. "I just enjoy being able to work with the dog, get him out here and find the stuff and get it out of here so it can't injure other soldiers," said Robbins.

Once the soldiers had collected, accounted for, and photographed the cache, all the ordnance was piled into the buildings. Once approval was given, ordnance disposal specialists went to work preparing explosives to destroy the weapons, training aids, and the buildings themselves. The mission came to an end as the charges went off, destroying the buildings and everything inside. Their

mission now complete, the soldiers waited for their ride back to the base.

One of the Black Hawk pilots, Chief Warrant Officer Mark Prosser, said, "It was kind of nice to be able to have one of the soldiers who discovered the site be on board the aircraft while we went out and did the mission. The thing I enjoy most about this type of mission is we're going to try to destroy munitions that could possibly be used for IEDs later on. So, the ground troops that we're supporting are actually going out there to blow up weapons caches that could be used against them later on." One of the helicopter crew members, Sgt. Matt Youst, was one of the soldiers who had originally reported the suspicious site while flying over the area earlier that week.

Clearing Sadr City

Members of the 82nd Airborne Division's 2nd Brigade Combat Team and the 3rd Stryker Brigade Combat Team, 2nd Infantry Division, based out of Camp Liberty, Iraq, conducted security operations with their Iraqi counterparts: a combined force of Iraqi police, national police, and Multi-national Division-Baghdad (MND) troops in the eastern Baghdad Sadr City district.

Sadr City is a stronghold of Muqtada Al Sadr, the extremist leader of rogue elements known for extrajudicial killings and attacks against coalition forces. Although Sadr City was the home of the Iraqi insurgent, some of the locals actually appeared happy to see the Iraqi and coalition soldiers arrive. Upon receiving smiles and waves by the children, Maj. Gen. Joseph Fil Jr., the commanding general of the MND, commented, "It's a promising first start. We sense there is an opportunity opening here that we want to immediately take advantage of while working with the Iraqi Security Forces and the people of Sadr City. Although much too early to tell, we sense that the people of the city are ready for a change."

At the conclusion of the security operations, a joint security station was established in the district police station for Sadr City. This security station allows a twenty-four-hour presence in the district and facilitates coordination between all security forces.

Operation Jalil

The operation was called Operation Jalil, in honor of Col. Jalil Nahi Hasoun, Samarra's former police chief, who was killed on 6 May 2007 during a suicide car bomb attack. Operating in Samarra, Iraq, soldiers of Company C, 2nd Battalion, 505th Parachute Infantry Regiment, have been patrolling and conducting operations. The paratroopers have supported the Iraqi Security Forces in a clearing operation to purge the city of the al-Qaeda presence that is terrorizing Samarra and its citizens.

The operation was led Maj. Gen. Rashid al-Helfy, commander of Iraqi Security Forces in Samarra. His men and paratroopers of Company C discovered weapons caches and bomb-making materials and detained more than eighty suspected terrorists, including suspects responsible for the 13 June 2007 bombing of the Askirya Mosque. The mosque, also known as the Golden Dome Shrine, was first bombed on 22 February 2006, which sparked a wave of sectarian violence throughout the country. The explosion collapsed the dome. A bombing on 13 June 2007 destroyed the two remaining minarets flanking the former dome.

Since then, more than twenty-five hundred Iraqi soldiers from the 4th Iraqi Army, and policemen from the 6th National Police Division, had been deployed to the city to create a stable security condition. Including Operation Jalil, Company C has also detained more than two hundred insurgents since the attack on the mosque in June.

According to Capt. Buddy Ferris, commander of Company C, "When the Iraqi national police first arrived in Samarra, they received anything but a warm welcome. The people of Samarra were very hesitant to receive the policemen. Now the citizens of Samarra are very receptive to the national police, and the paratroopers from Company C have seen this through the vast amount of information they receive every day from the people in Samarra about terrorists operating in their neighborhoods. The paratroopers like to see that the Iraqis are taking the lead. We will continue to push forward with the Iraqi security forces so they can provide a stable enough environment so we can start developing a legitimate government that functions and is tied in with the [Salah ad Din] province."

In 2005 the U.S. Army required an entire brigade to secure the city. Two years later a force of only 150 paratroopers was responsible for securing a city of more than 150,000 inhabitants. Since the paratroopers of Company C have been in Samarra, they have killed more than fifty terrorists and detained more than three hundred. "[The paratroopers] have been holding the lid on the city of Samarra. This company has been able to hold Samarra in one piece, so to speak, and has actually been able to make progress and it speaks volumes," said Ferris.

As the United States continues to conduct the war against Islamofacism around the globe, the 82nd Airborne Division will continue to be America's Guard of Honor. The men and women of the All American Division will be on call to bring the terrorists to justice or justice to them, Airborne—All The Way!

Acknowledgments

First, I acknowledge God as the author of liberty; may He continue to bless our great nation with peace. I thank Steve Gansen, editor, Zenith Press; Harry Sarles, Army Public Affairs, New York; Monica Manganaro, Public Affairs Office, Fort Benning; Capt. Kinal Sztalkoper, Fort Benning; Maj. Thomas Earnhardt, Public Affairs Office, Fort Bragg; Jimmie Hallis, 82nd Airborne Museum, Fort Bragg; U.S. Army Institute of Heraldry; 1st Sgt. Albert Hinton and Sgt. 1st Class William Johnson, NCOIC, Advanced Airborne School, Fort Bragg; Defend America; Digital Video and Imagery Distribution System Images and assorted interviews—Spc. Amanda Morrissey and Sgt. Michael Pryor, 2nd Brigade Combat Team, 82nd Airborne Division Public Affairs; Sgt. Tony J. Spain and Staff Sgt. Matthew Acosta, 22nd Mobile Public Affairs Detachment; Pfc. Aubree Rundle, Task Force Pegasus Public Affairs; 2nd Lt. Eric Williams, Task Force Corsair; Petty Officer 1st Class Scott Cohen, Combined Security Transition Command, Afghanistan Public Affairs; Master Sgt. Dave Larsen, 1st Cavalry Division Public Affairs; Sgt. Tony White, 5th Mobile Public Affairs Detachment; Pfc. James Wilt, 82nd Airborne Division Public Affairs Office, Task Force "White Falcon"; Sgt. Joshua R. Ford, 3rd Brigade Combat Team, 82nd Airborne Division Public Affairs; Spc. Matthew Leary, Task Force Fury Public Affairs Office; Sgt. Gregory Heath, 4th Public Affairs Detachment; Spc. Daniel Bearl, 25th Combat Aviation Brigade; Defense Visual Information Center.

Glossary

ANA: Afghan National Army

ANSF: Afghan National Security Force

AO: area of operations

BCT: brigade combat team

downrange: physically in a combat zone

GWOT: global war on terrorism

HMMWV or Humvee: high-mobility multipurpose wheeled vehicle

ISAF: International Security Assistance Force in country: physically in a combat zone; see also "downrange"

KIA: killed in action

MRE: meal ready to eat

NATO: North Atlantic Treaty Organization

NCO: noncommissioned officer: an enlisted person with command responsibility over soldiers of lesser rank; a corporal (grade E4) or any grade of sergeant (grades E5 to E9); see also "specialist"

PDF: Panamanian Defense Forces

PIR: parachute infantry regiment

PLF: parachute landing fall

RPG: rocket-propelled grenade

klick: kilometer; 0.6214 mile

Ma Deuce: Browning .50-caliber machine gun; the weapon's designation is M2

SEALs: Sea/Air/Land (U.S. Navy commandos)

SERE: survival, escape, resistance, and evasion

trooper: used in lieu of "soldier" when referring to Airborne soldiers

WIA: wounded in action

Index

Other **Zenith Press** titles of interest:

**U.S. AIR FORCE
SPECIAL OPS**
ISBN 978-0-7603-2947-8

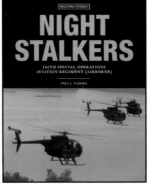

NIGHT STALKERS
ISBN 978-0-7603-2141-8

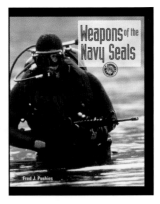

**WEAPONS OF THE
NAVY SEALS**
ISBN 978-0-7603-1790-9

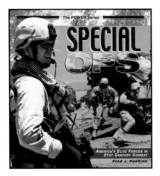

SPECIAL OPS
ISBN 978-0-7603-1603-1

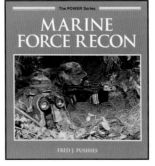

**MARINE
FORCE RECON**
ISBN 978-0-7603-1011-4

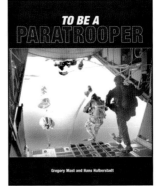

**TO BE A
PARATROOPER**
ISBN 978-0-7603-3046-8

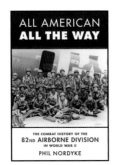

**ALL AMERICAN,
ALL THE WAY**
ISBN 978-0-7603-2201-5

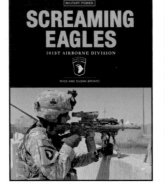

SCREAMING EAGLES
ISBN 978-0-7603-3122-7

RED FLAG
ISBN 978-0-7603-2530-8

ZENITH PRESS

Find us on the internet at **www.ZenithPress.com**